by Marcia Blitz

Harmony Books/New York

Acknowledgments

Chronicling the life of Donald Duck would have been difficult for me without the cheerful help of the Disney Studio (in particular Merrie Lasky, Dave Smith, Wendall Mohler, May Weigele, Jeanette Kroger), impossible without the initial faith of publisher Bruce Harris. Working on *Donald* would have been much less fun without my editor, Manuela Soares, and designer Ken Sansone.

Finally, writing the book would have been a grim experience without the support and encouragement of family and friends. Thanks to all those who suddenly became Duck-conscious, engaged in provocative discussions of Donald, and kept my spirits and inspiration high with an assortment of Duck memorabilia.

Most of all, I'd like to thank Susan Petersen. She is mentor, friend, "wonderfulness" personified.

—M.H.B.

Printed in the United States of America.
Published simultaneously in Canada by General Publishing Company Limited.
Designed by Ken Sansone.

Library of Congress Cataloging in Publication Data

Blitz, Marcia.
  Donald Duck.

  Filmography: p. 229
  Bibliography: p. 253

  1. Donald Duck (Cartoon character)   2. Disney (Walt)
Productions—History.   I. Title.
NC1766.U52D532   1979   741.5'973   78-73705
ISBN 0-517-52961-0

Contents

"Thank heaven for Donald Duck!"
—Trevor Howard in *Brief Encounter*

Introducktion

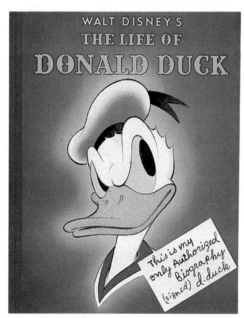

Donald Duck's first biography, published in the thirties, was by no means definitive.

Donald Duck was created in 1934 at the Walt Disney Studios in Burbank, California. His first appearance, in one of Disney's Silly Symphonies, introduced Donald as a tall, gawky, thoroughly selfish and ill-tempered duck. But there was something very special about this particular duck, and Donald quickly went on to become one of Mickey Mouse's co-stars. Mickey was already a national hero, but Walt Disney felt that Mickey was limited in his role as boy-next-door and needed a volatile co-star like Donald in his cartoons.

Donald's status as co-star soon catapulted him to stardom of his own. In the forties, Donald was America's favorite war hero, turning out films to help the war effort just like the other top stars. In the fifties and sixties Donald successfully made the switch to television, capturing the hearts of an entire generation of American youth. This daring duck has become a star of international fame in the seventies. His cartoons and comics are shown and read throughout the world, and fan clubs for Donald abound.

Donald's physical appearance changed during his early years. After his initial appearance, Donald took shape as an adorably round, pure white fowl. He grew shorter, but retained his blue sailor suit and hat, and added a little swagger to his step. Donald's voice (courtesy of Clarence Nash) retained the harsh raspiness that made it enchanting to millions.

Unlike Mickey, who was sweet and sensitive, Donald was prone to incredible rages and unforgivable selfishness. Yet it is these raw human characteristics and his basic human impulses that draw us to him. Donald's tantrums and explosions became his trademark, but he tempered them with determination and courage. In addition to those qualities, Donald could exhibit an incredible childlike innocence and shyness. Donald looked like a duck, but acted like a human and it was an irresistible combination.

Donald's personality was as unique in the animation of the thirties and forties as it is today. We love him for his gloriously unrepressed character; we envy his straightforward way of dealing with the world; we applaud his devil-may-care attitude; and we revel in the power of his rages. Whether he's being hotheaded or selfish, understanding or kind, we respond to Donald. His range of emotion is endless, and it has made him one of the most popular characters in the history of animation.

For over forty years Donald Duck has brought immeasurable joy to audiences all over the world, regardless of age or nationality. And now it's time to recapture that joy—to giggle, guffaw, and linger over Donald's finest moments in film, television, and comics. So, fans of the fine-feathered film star, turn the page. As Walt Disney proclaimed in 1960, "This is your life, Donald Duck."

The Men
Behind the Duck

The dashing young Walt Disney took up polo in his spare time. Soon after, in 1936, *Mickey's Polo Team* was released.

ince 1934, Donald Duck has reigned as the world's most illustrious fowl. Both young and old cheer his cartoons and comics; critics review and analyze him as if he were as real a star as Robert Redford; millions of kids and adults pay tribute to him by imitating his voice; products from pillows to sneakers bear his wide-eyed grinning image. It all started for Donald with a friendly rival named Mickey Mouse—for it was Mickey who brought out the best (which was often the worst) in Donald, and who gave him The Big Break into Show Biz.

In 1934, when Donald was hatched in Walt Disney's imagination, Mickey Mouse was firmly established as one of the world's superstars. The Disney Studio, although still small by today's standards, welcomed all who entered with an imposing sign that read: *Mickey Mouse Silly Symphonies Sound Cartoons.* Then, as now, the name Walt Disney was a household word.

But it didn't happen overnight.

alter Elias Disney was born in Chicago on December 5, 1901, and by the time he was eight his family had moved to Kansas City. In his early childhood, he dutifully worked on a paper route and later as a "candy butcher" on the Santa Fe Railroad, but he always showed much more of a preference—and a talent—for drawing. In 1919, after serving in a Red Cross ambulance unit in France, young Disney returned to Kansas City, hoping to become a commercial artist. He got work with a local art firm, but was laid off after only a few months, when the busy Christmas season was over. He then formed his own commercial art company with his talented colleague Ub Iwerks (pronounced "Eye-works"). They wisely called the firm Iwerks–Disney Commercial Artists, instead of Disney–Iwerks, which, Disney thought, might have had people calling up about their glasses.

After a short time, however, Disney left the business for the Kansas City Film Ad Company. Several months later, Iwerks, who would become a major force in the early Disney Studio, joined him there. The move was a fateful step in the careers of both young men; it was there that they discovered animation and become totally fascinated and enchanted by the art.

It wasn't long before Walt was turning out his own crude but promising cartoons. Billed as "Newman Laugh-O-Grams" (for the Newman Theater, where they were shown), they were humorous shorts commenting on life in Kansas City. Soon the "Newman" was dropped as the enterprising Walt hired other artists and formed his own Laugh-O-Gram Films Co., Inc. They produced a series of updated fairy tales (including *Cinderella, Jack and the Beanstalk, Puss 'n' Boots*) that were good but did not do as well as Disney expected. When a potential distributor went bankrupt, the undaunted animator realized that there was

nothing left for him in the Midwest. He decided that the best thing to do was to go elsewhere. The only place for him was Hollywood, where magic was becoming the major product.

Arriving there in 1923, Disney, now a twenty-one-year-old aspiring producer, brought with him a pilot for an original new series combining live action and animation—*Alice in Cartoonland*. When the doors remained closed in Hollywood, he signed the Alice comedies with a New York distributor. Within a few years, the comedies were selling at $1,800 an episode, and Alice became enough of a success to merit a bigger operation.

In 1926, the Walt Disney Studio on Hollywood's Hyperion Avenue opened for business. It was staffed by Walt's brother Roy (the businessman), Ub Iwerks, several animators, and a few women responsible for inking and painting. One of them, Lillian Bounds, would eventually become Disney's wife.

From there, it was on to bigger and better cartoons, usually counterbalanced by bigger and better troubles. His next venture, *Oswald the Lucky Rabbit*, became a dazzling, beloved, moneymaking hit—only to be spirited away by the contractual rights of the distributor, Charles Mintz.

1154-8073

ith Oswald gone, Disney was left to depend on his fertile imagination. So, remembering the little creatures that used to scurry around his Kansas City studio, he and Iwerks developed Oswald's brilliant successor, Mickey Mouse, who debuted in 1928 in *Steamboat Willie* (See *Mickey Mouse; Fifty Happy Years*, Harmony Books, 1977, for the full story), a cartoon that became a smashing, talking hit.

By the early thirties, to satisfy rampant Mousemania, the Disney Studio was turning out approximately eighteen Mouse cartoons a year. They were already being translated and shown all over the world, and the lucrative Disney merchandising empire was founded. Soon Mickey appeared on everything from notebooks to rattles to tea sets. In 1931, *Time* magazine devoted a feature article to the famous mouse, and although he wasn't Man (let alone Mouse) of the Year, he was immortalized in the waxworks of Madame Tussaud. Mickey won Hollywood's highest praise in the form of two Academy Award nominations in 1931 and 1933 (for *Mickey's Orphans* and *Building a Building*, respectively); and a special Oscar went to Disney in 1932, just for Mickey's creation.

The public, needless to say, was thronging to see the Mouse, first checking their Mickey Mouse watches to be sure they'd be on time. But back at the Disney Studio, the handwriting (mostly in animator's graphite pencil) was already on the wall. Even at the height of his popularity, Mickey's antics were somewhat limited by his character. Children loved him and adults warmed to him, but the problem with the ever-smiling Mickey was simply that he had grown *too* nice. Although he had started out as a troublemaker with a mean streak, he was now settling into his role as the boy next door. Where he used to engage in questionable antics, such as using a crane to pick Minnie up by her panties in *Steamboat Willie*, he was now expected to act with the moral integrity befitting a symbol of America. In the beginning Mickey was surprising and delightful. He was still delightful, but he had become predictable.

Jack Hannah, who spent thirty years in the Disney Studio as animator, writer, and director, has summed up Mickey's essential problem: "We began to have an awful hard time finding stories for Mickey...[he] began as a mischief-maker, but he developed right off the bat into a little hero type, and you couldn't knock him around too much."

Walt himself recognized the difficulty of sustaining interest in his creation. A few years later he would comment: "Mickey's our problem child. He's so much of an institution that we're limited in what we can do with him. If we have Mickey kicking someone in the pants, we get a million letters from mothers telling us we're giving their kids wrong ideas. Mickey must always be sweet, always lovable. What can you do with such a leading man?"

The lovable Mickey Mouse. A few years after his creation, Disney writers and animators found the perfect foil for Mickey in Donald Duck.

One Hollywood legend dates Friday, March 13, as Donald Duck's birthday. Here he is as he appeared on that day. According to astrology, that would make the Duck a Fish (Pisces). This sign is characterized by slyness, moodiness, and chronic discontent. The *official* date for Donald's birthday is June 9, 1934.

Opposite: The Big Bang Theory, in which Donald bursts forth fully grown and ready to take on the world.

Even in 1932, Disney knew that the answer to his question was to complement Mickey with less straitlaced characters. He continued to try to make the Mouse cartoons fresh and exciting by placing him in unusual locales (South Sea, Alps, African deserts). In the early thirties, Walt was also concentrating on a new art form he called his Silly Symphonies. It was in one of them (*The Wise Little Hen*) that Donald Duck—the outrageous antithesis to Mickey—made his small but well-noted debut.

As is so often the case with cinematic greats, the true story of Donald's beginnings has become obscured by legend. Several conflicting stories circulate from Hollywood to New York, but which you believe hardly matters once you've encountered him.

The most mythical version of Donald's genesis comes directly from the Disney Studio. (One must remember that in Disneyland, anything is possible.) The following statement was made in an issue of *Disneynews*—a fitting origin for Donald, even down to the birth date.

Legend has it that Donald Duck came into being one stormy night in March—on a Friday the 13th to be exact. It is said that he flew into a window at the Disney studios disguised as a mud puddle and completely disrupted a story meeting with his belligerent, "Do ya wanna fight?"

A sketch from *The Wise Little Hen* (1934)
depicting the dilapidated houseboat
where Donald was found dancing a
hornpipe. This is the first known drawing
of Donald Duck.

This story certainly sounds plausible to anyone who knows
Donald's tactics, but today there is no one left at Disney who
can verify this incident. Another story on record relates
Donald's "birth" to a similar unfortunate habit of butting in.

In 1935, a reporter named Dana Burnet, interviewing
Disney for *Pictorial Review*, asked how he got the idea for
drawing a duck character for the screen. Walt denied that
Donald was *ever* just an idea—he insisted over and over that
"he was always a talking duck." He then went on to relate this
little-known story concerning the first historic meeting of
Mickey and Donald:

*You see, Mickey and his gang had been asked to broadcast on
one of the N.B.C. programs. It meant a lot of extra work for the
Mouse, but he decided to oblige. Well, Mickey was up there at
the mike, doing his stuff, when this duck came along and butted
in. The duck had learned a piece and wanted to recite it. He
kept crowding up to the mike and trying to recite "Mary Had a
Little Lamb." Well, you know how Mickey is. Always ready to
give a guy a break. But he was afraid that Donald would spoil
his broadcast, so he shoved him away, and the duck kept
coming back and squawking "Mary Had a Little Lamb" into the
mike...*

At this point, the reporter stopped Disney to question him
further. He never continued this particular story and perhaps
that's why it's faded into legend. There is one element in Walt's
account that does appear in the more widely accepted stories.
The link is "Mary Had a Little Lamb." It is certain that the
children's poem was Donald's original audition piece.

In another version of the story, as Disney would tell it in later years, he discovered his prize-winning duck much as the other movie moguls were discovering starlets in drugstores. One day Disney turned on the radio and heard "Whistling Clarence, the Adohr Birdman" in the middle of one of his animal imitations. The "birdman" was immediately summoned to the Disney Studio and asked to put his talent to work for the character of a nameless talking duck.

To be fair, in Walt's eyes that *was* the way it happened. But unbeknownst to him (perhaps someone was too busy to tell him,) the animal impressionist was never actually called to the Studio. "Whistling Clarence" became the world's most recognizable voice through a remarkable and happy coincidence. His story gives us the definitive account of how Donald Duck came to the screen.

In 1933, as a recent immigrant to California, twenty-nine-year-old Clarence Nash was promoting the Adohr Milk Company by driving a miniature milk wagon pulled by miniature horses. He had been hired by the company when they discovered his talent for animal imitations. A large part of the job was entertaining children. Sometime before he had started driving, however, Nash had appeared on a radio show called "The Merry Makers." In order to placate a friend who hadn't heard him perform in a while, he went on once more and did a free show (unheard of in the Depression). What Nash didn't know was that his pay for the appearance would ultimately be more than the station could ever have afforded. As luck would have it, this was the show that Disney had tuned into. But it wasn't until some weeks later that Nash discovered Disney's interest in him.

Usually, Nash's daily route did not take him past the Disney Studio, but one day he just found himself on Hyperion Avenue and partly on impulse, partly because friends had urged him to go there, knocked on Mickey Mouse's door. Although still wearing his milkman's outfit, he got an interview with director Wilfred Jackson. He performed his baby chickens, turkeys, dogs, birds—even his raccoons and coyotes. Unfortunately for Nash, there was no overwhelming response—until he recited "Mary Had a Little Lamb" in the voice of a character he had always called Mary. "When I started to recite it," Nash remembers, "Jackson secretly switched on the intercom that went to Walt's office. Disney raced in, listened to me some more, and cried excitedly, 'Stop! Stop! That's our talking duck!'"

And so it was that Donald Duck was actually born. "Ducky" (as Nash came to be called) looks back on the moment with both nostalgia and amusement. Rather than being insulted that his "Mary" voice was taken for a duck's, he was happy to get the work. "Fortunately for me" he says, "Walt heard me quack like a duck *after* I did the 'Mary' recitation!"

Just Ducky. Clarence Nash records a Donald Duck solo for one of the 133 Duck cartoons and specials. For more than forty years, Nash has been the one and only voice of Donald Duck. A 1978 poll of high school students found Donald No. 3 on a list of favorite imitations—right after John Travolta and the Czech Brothers of *Saturday Night Live*.

"I wanted to be a doctor, but as it turned out I was bound to be the biggest quack in the country."

—Clarence "Ducky" Nash

Ducky was a mandolin player in the Alamo Quintet and an animal impressionist when he toured on the Redpath Chautauqua and Lyceum circuit in the twenties.

Clarence Nash, a native of Watonga, Oklahoma, was born on December 7, 1904, three years before Oklahoma even became a state. He grew up on a farm, surrounded by animals, and it was inevitable that he would start to imitate them. When he was nine, his family moved to Glasgow, Missouri, and the year after that to a town that is now part of Independence. It was there that Nash discovered a curious practice among his schoolmates.

"It was a big thing for the kids to try to outdo one another imitating animal sounds," he remembers. "By the time I was twelve, I could do the sounds of dogs, cats, baby chicks, horses, pigs, raccoons, baby coyotes, and a lot of birds." But all that was before he acquired his final childhood pet—a baby billy goat.

"The goat was only a couple days old," says Nash. "I had to feed it with a baby bottle, and when I stopped feeding it it would cry like a frightened little girl." Naturally young Nash was intrigued by the challenge of a new sound. He learned to imitate that unique bleating and eventually started to put words into that voice.

During the next year he used his impressions to amaze kids in the school yard, until one day, a school talent show prompted him to bring his voices before the general public. In his newfound goat voice he recited "Mary Had a Little Lamb"—and as the wild applause from the audience died down, he claims he heard a voice whisper in his ear, "That's a voice you're going to use someday."

Someday, perhaps, but not right away. Clarence was still a stagestruck high school kid in Kansas City, Missouri, and would later drop out of school to tour the Midwest as a mandolin player and animal impressionist on the Redpath Chautauqua and Lyceum circuit. (These were vaudeville shows that had evolved from religious and educational programs into entertainment.) It seemed to him, as it did to so many others, that vaudeville would go on forever, but his life was irrevocably changed by the Chautauquas' demise in the late twenties.

By 1930 Nash had married his sweetheart, Margie, promising that he would give up show business, settle down, and get a "normal" job. The quest for that elusive work took them first to San Francisco and then to Los Angeles. When it became apparent that there was no "normal" work in Los Angeles either, Nash was lucky to get the spot on "The Merry Makers" radio show to do his animal impressions. That led to the promotional job with the milk company and to the extraordinary coincidences that made Nash the voice of Donald Duck.

Opposite: **From the private collection of Clarence Nash, a 1918 photo of Mary, the world's only known "billy duck." Mary's unusual bleating inspired the voice that came to be Donald's. Mary died several years later and was laid to rest by a tearful Nash.**

The voices of nephews Huey, Dewey, and Louie were also recorded by Nash.

Opposite, above: **Ducky Nash as "Whistling Clarence, the Adohr Birdman."** *Opposite below:* **Walt never animated Mickey, but he provided the character's voice until the late 1940s. Here, enjoying their roles as cartoon stars, Disney and Nash record dialogue between Mickey and Donald.**

According to Frank Thomas, an animator at Disney, Ducky need not have worried because Donald's success was assured from the moment Nash opened his mouth. Thomas explains that to create and draw the best, most vivid cartoon character, animators need a voice that suggests attitudes and expressions. "We've had fine and famous actors come and do voices and I couldn't see anything. Ducky, with this crazy quack of his—you really believed it."

On December 2, 1933, Clarence Nash became Disney's 125th employee. (There are now more than 20,000.) It was an association that was to be long and happy, lasting through 128 Duck cartoons and five full-length features. While under contract to do Donald, Nash's enormous talents were also used in a variety of other roles. His credits range from ducks on film to Audio-Animatronics in the theme parks—including the voices of Huey, Dewey, and Louie, Daisy, Mickey, Jiminy Cricket (after the death of Cliff Edwards), a bullfrog in *Bambi*, dogs in *101 Dalmatians*, and birds in the Tiki Room at Disneyland.

In the very beginning, Nash was a natural, although raw, talent, and as much as Disney liked the voice, he still felt there was room for improvement. Throughout his career, Ducky was continually making modifications in the voice. Sometimes they were subtle, but as the years went by Donald Duck became noticeably better.

The first, most pressing voice problem facing Nash was the choice of a vocabulary that would ensure that Donald could be understood; he could not be totally unintelligible. There were certain words—such as licorice—that proved a formidable challenge and had to be practiced again and again.

Another thorny problem posed to Ducky in the thirties was a censorship system far more stringent than today's. "You couldn't have said 'Nuts!' audibly in the thirties," remembers Ducky. "We tried it once and were forced to dub in 'I give up.'" Sometimes it did work out to Nash's advantage, though. Animator Frank Thomas recalls: "Ducky's voice really teased you. You understood just enough. And you could really get by a censor."

Ducky's most difficult voice challenge presented itself when Donald Duck cartoons were released abroad and they all had to be dubbed in foreign languages. "Words were written out for me phonetically and I learned to quack in French ('couac'), Spanish, Portuguese, Japanese, Chinese (Yes, Peking Duck!), and German. (For some reason, German was the hardest.) Then I'd listen to the English dialogue over earphones and match the length and mood of the dialogue in the foreign language. It was critical to get everything down pat so they wouldn't have to reanimate."

Even after the famous voice had taken form, there were still developments to be made in Donald's character. An admiring

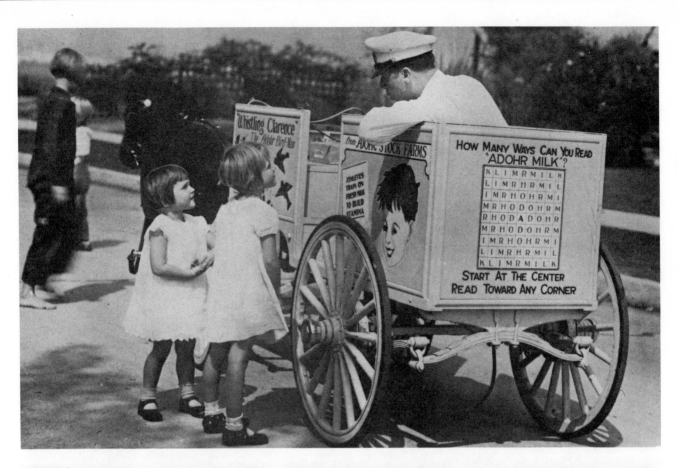

In a scene from *The Reluctant Dragon* (1941), author/humorist Robert Benchley visits the Disney Studio and gets a squawking lesson from Ducky.

Nash credits Disney with the suggestions for some of the most important aspects of Donald Duck's personality—such as the volatile temper and the infectious laugh—but Ducky was always delighted to contribute story ideas himself. It was Ducky, for instance, who suggested that Donald express a sensitive, artistic side. "I figured that if a duck could talk, why not sing? I was always a music fan and opera intrigued me." Thus, in *Mickey's Grand Opera, Old MacDonald Duck, Donald's Garden,* and other cartoons, the Duck got to sing his heart out. (In *Donald's Dilemma,* his voice remarkably changed to that of a honey-voiced crooner, but only after he had been hit on the head with a flowerpot and forgot who he was!) In recent years, Ducky has expressed the wish that the Studio make one last Duck picture in which Donald would do nothing but sing grand opera.

For most of his career, like others behind the scenes at Disney, Clarence Nash's true identity was unknown to the public. Disney insisted that anonymity sustained the illusion of fantasy in his cartoons and felt that if credits were shown at the end, they would introduce a jarring note of reality. As a result of this policy, audiences could only speculate about the man behind Donald. Rumors abounded that Mel Blanc, known to be the voice of Bugs Bunny, was also the voice of Donald Duck.

Ducky received credit in other ways, though. He claims that Donald's renown and the audience's laughter have been more than enough reward for him. He's also had the unexpected payment of sweet—though harmless—revenge through Donald. It happened when he once went on a tour of the Cave of the Winds and recognized his guide as his high school principal. He began a loud, steady quacking that could be heard all over the cave. The much-perturbed guide was powerless to quiet Nash in this setting—even though he had once made a practice of keeping Nash after school for imitating animals instead of doing arithmetic.

For the past forty years, Clarence Nash has been able to spread the joy of Donald Duck in person—whether he's formally entertaining or giving interviews or surprising children in supermarkets. He first went on the road sometime around 1940 with a two-foot-high papier-mâché doll (Donald's no dummy!) given to him by the Studio for the purpose of touring. The raucous twosome has entertained everywhere—especially at school assemblies, hospitals, and orphanages. The Donald who travels with Nash today is not the original model. Number Four doll, made out of fiberglass, is unbreakable, wear-resistant, dressed in drip-dry clothes, and equipped with a specially designed Samsonite case.

It must be revealed here that there were some other ducks in Nash's life—ducks of the non-Disney kind. He sometimes appeared on the "Burns and Allen" radio show, playing Gracie's emotional, but inarticulate pet duck, Herman. (His contract with Disney forbade him to *talk* duck with anyone else, he could only quack!) He also quacked for comedian Bob Burns and cowboy Gene Autry, but obviously neither of those fowl characters could hold a feather to Donald, since they have vanished into oblivion.

Although Donald left the screen, except for reruns, in 1961, the jovial *un*cantankerous Ducky Nash, at seventy-four, is alive and well and happily retired in Glendale, California. From time to time, he still makes local appearances as Donald, and he was called back to the Studio a few years ago to record the opening sequence of the New Mickey Mouse Club. ("Mickey Mouse ...DONALD DUCK!") In all these years, he hasn't lost one tiny bit of Donald's original glory; the voice is still animated with gusto, gutsiness, and mischief.

For all his vocal renown, however, Ducky has largely remained a private person. The 5-foot 2-inch body attached to the world's most famous voice can go virtually unnoticed anywhere outside the Studio. A little girl to whom Ducky once quacked "Hi" worriedly asked him why he was talking like Donald Duck. He replied that he didn't know. But when Nash is introduced, children giggle and adults wax nostalgic.... And then there was the waitress who must have been so excited that she made an unfortunate choice of metaphors.

"Mr. Nash, you're the cat's meow," she said.

On one of his many tours, Clarence Nash gets ready to entertain with an early model of Donald.

Hey, Kids!
Wanna Talk Like Me?

Astound your friends! Be a hit at parties! Here, straight from the Duck's mouth and for the first time in print, are Clarence Nash's step-by-step instructions for Donald's voice:

1

Put your tongue to the roof of your mouth

2

Twist tongue a little to left

3

Press tongue

4

"Vibrate" tongue

5

Form words just like using your own voice

With just a few hours of practice, you can be quacking everyone up!

The Supporting Player

The Silly Symphony series was among Disney's first artistic triumphs. *Flowers and Trees* was the first cartoon to be made with the new three-color process.

In the spring of 1929 the country was introduced to a new Walt Disney phenomenon. At the Roxy Theater in New York, audiences delighted to four dancing skeletons who had risen from the grave to cavort among the tombstones. The music was appropriately haunting, the characters grim but comedic. And although this was a cartoon that Disney's distributor had refused to handle ("Stick to Mickey Mouse," he said), *The Skeleton Dance*, the first Silly Symphony, was a wildly resounding success. It was just one of the many times that Disney had gone out on a limb to play his hunch. As usual, he was correct; never again did he have to distribute a Silly Symphony himself.

The ten-year series of Silly Symphonies came about for several reasons. They were a natural extension of the growing musical sophistication at the Disney Studio and a result of Disney's genius coupled with his insatiable desire to experiment and innovate. By this time Disney had long since stopped drawing himself to take on the more important task of providing the creative direction around the Studio. He would supervise artists, be present at recording and gag sessions, and, more often than not, add the one brilliant touch that would pull everything together.

The Silly Symphonies were the idea of Disney's first composer, Carl Stalling. It is to Disney's credit that he produced them, giving audiences of the thirties an unprecedented experience in music and animation. A similar reaction was not to be felt again in movie theaters for many years—until the sixties and seventies and the era of revolutionary science-fiction special effects.

What audiences were responding to so enthusiastically was not merely comedy or adventure; the structure of the early Symphonies lacked a narrative plot as a rule. Instead, these amazing creations centered around a mood-setting theme such as "Winter" or "Spring," and music provided the inspiration for the art, with compositions ranging from classical pieces to original scores by Stalling.

Success came and Disney should have been happy. But as lyrical and technically good as the earliest Symphonies were, he was obsessed with making them better. In 1932, it was a Silly Symphony that caused an industry sensation and made animation history: *Flowers and Trees* was the first cartoon ever to be made in Technicolor's new three-color process.

From that point on, the Symphonies scored triumph after triumph. They did not appear to solve Disney's problem of finding fresh characters to reinforce Mickey, but they were gradually evolving into cartoons with plots.

At last, in 1934, came *The Wise Little Hen*—another adaption of a well-known Aesop tale. Disney had already discovered Ducky and was finally ready to put him to use. Ducky's actual voice work on Donald's first appearance probably amounted to a matter of minutes.

A model sheet from *The Wise Little Hen* shows Donald's size in relation to the other characters.

T he *Wise Little Hen* introduced a character who today is definitely recognizable, but whose long gangly body with its rubbery neck, extended bill, and feathery fingers (*see* sketches) gives him an entirely different aura. Donald, as first drawn by Disney animators Art Babbitt and Dick Huemer, looks cruder, less expressive. Until he fell into the hands of animator Fred Spencer and later director Jack Hannah, he was more of a caricature than a character.

Fortunately, Donald's original appearance had little to do with his initial success. In his first modest role, he was noticeable enough to draw fan mail—a sure sign that a star was in the making. He made his debut wearing his familiar sailor suit with its matching hat and sounding off in the quack that no real duck could ever come close to. But most of all, he played the part with his splendidly characteristic ill-temperedness— arriving on the animation scene loudly and *literally* bellyaching.

Overleaf: A separate model sheet made for the Duck shows him dancing, smiling, and bellyaching. One question has been raised repeatedly about Donald's appearance: Why does the American Duck wear a French sailor's cap?

Donald Duck

"WISE LITTLE HEN" U.S. 20.

The Wise Little Hen wised up when she met the unscrupulous likes of Peter Pig and Donald Duck.

Below: A working sketch from the same cartoon indicating action.

As *The Wise Little Hen* opens, a mother hen and her chicks are looking for someone to help them plant their corn. They first go to see Peter Pig and politely explain their predicament. The pig, a lazy, good-for-nothing creature, is more than unsympathetic. He dramatically refuses her, pleading a painful stomachache. The hen goes on. She nears a river where there is a dilapidated houseboat, and there on the deck is Donald dancing a hornpipe. The hen is hoping that Donald will want to help her with the planting and puts the question to him. His first big moment on screen is his graceless refusal with this immortal line of dialogue: "Who—me? Oh, no! I got a belly-ache!"

By the end of the cartoon, Donald's and Peter's mischief has been punished. The two shifty characters shamelessly ask to share the food they were too lazy to gather. But the hen "rewards" them with a liberal dose of castor oil, giving Donald some real misery—and a further reason for some loud and vehement squawks.

The rest, as they say in Donald's hometown of Duckburg, is history—although at the time Disney, the animators, and Ducky did not realize what a "monster" they had created.

Soon after *The Wise Little Hen*, an article about the Disney family appeared in *Time* magazine. It pointed out in no uncertain terms just how uncertain Donald's future actually was. "Last year two new characters, Donald Duck and Clara Cluck, were admitted into the family group, on trial. If they win public favor they will be formally adopted into the family. If not, back they go, to appear infrequently in a Silly Symphony."

" WHO ME ? OH NO !
I GOT A BELLY ACHE. "

Something to sneeze at. Donald's performance in *Orphan's Benefit* **elicits a rousing round of Bronx cheers.**

Obviously, an enthusiastic public gave Donald an overwhelming mandate. Never again was the scene-stealing squawker to be relegated to a bit part. His next role put him directly on center stage and gave him the opportunity for nothing less than a bravura performance. He was still just one among several acts, but as punsters over the years have noted on many occasions, Donald filled the bill.

In his second smash appearance, the Duck entertained in *Orphan's Benefit*, a 1934 black-and-white Mickey Mouse cartoon (later remade in color) in which Mickey, Goofy, and Donald appear together for the first time. The plot is a hilarious treatment of the antagonism between a performer and a jeering audience of hecklers. With our dauntless Duck as the running joke in the show, the laughs come easy and often.

As the curtain rises before a houseful of look-alike little mice, Mickey Mouse, the evening's master of ceremonies, enters to deafening applause and cheers. Donald, in the wings, has apparently taken this for his cue and comes darting out on stage, putting a quick end to Mickey's song-and-dance act. A few stray catcalls (if that's the term when they're done by mice) are heard, but they don't bother the Duck...yet.

Two of the mischievous orphans take aim at the unsuspecting Donald.

Opposite: **A poster for the 1941 color remake of** *Orphan's Benefit.*

With great emotion and accompanying histrionics, Donald starts to recite "Mary Had a Little Lamb" and "Little Boy Blue," only to stop when he forgets his lines. Whoops of laughter issue from the audience, and as quiet returns one of the little "angels" blows his nose. The temperamental performer mistakes the honking for the old raspberry and starts to mutter and quack in indignation. The mice, having gotten a good idea, let blast an entire symphony of Bronx cheers from beneath their handkerchiefs. Donald, in turn, responds with growing fury. His fists are clenched, the curses fly . . . but suddenly he's removed by the hook!

Next there is a dancing interlude from Clarabelle Cow, Horace Horsecollar, and Pluto—just enough time for Donald to regain his cool and formulate a plan. He returns to the stage, smiling with a deceptive sweetness, and then assaults the orphans' ears with a loud and annoying Bronx-cheer trumpet. Instead of being taps for the night, it becomes a clarion call to all-out war. By the time this segment is over, Donald has been bombed by an ice-cream cone and pummeled by ingeniously propelled boxing gloves. The hook once again mercifully removes him from the arena of combat, while the mice devote their "attention" to the operatic wonder, Clara Cluck.

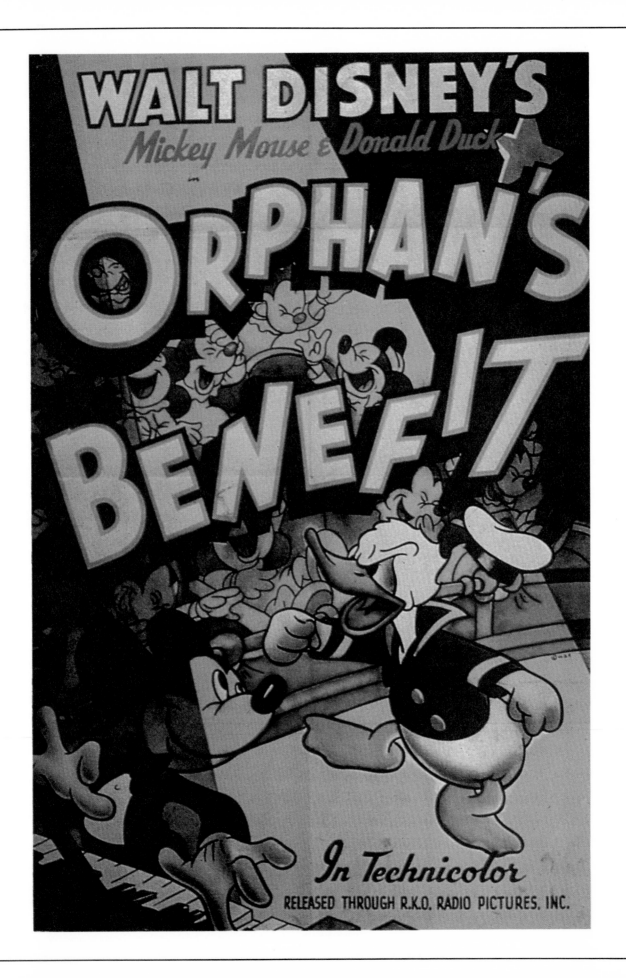

At last, Donald brings the house down—flowerpots, bricks, and all.

And then it is time for the final round. Donald returns looking furious, the steam almost palpable in the air. For a minute the orphans feign innocent interest and Donald believes that he's triumphed. But in a matter of seconds, he goes down under a barrage of balloon-lofted bricks and eggs.

It can be seen that the framework of *Orphan's Benefit* was traditionally slapstick. Audiences laughed at Donald's physical mishaps much as they laughed at Chaplin's or Keaton's. But in this instance there was the added dimension of Donald's abrasive personality. Surely nothing like it had ever been seen in a cartoon.

In the early thirties, when cartoons were at their height, the animated world was a densely populated one. Felix the Cat had been on the scene for some fifteen years and was often seen in the company of such figures as Koko the Klown, Mutt and Jeff, Popeye, Betty Boop, and Disney's own Oswald the Lucky Rabbit. Except for Mickey, none of these cartoon characters could come close to the universal appeal of Donald, and it would be almost another ten years until the stiffest competition—especially Bugs Bunny and Woody Woodpecker—would come from Warner Brothers, MGM, Screen Gems, and Walter Lantz.

In the beginning, Donald Duck was far from the complex, intriguing, and sympathetic character he would later become. Since he had been created to accommodate the plot of *The Wise Little Hen,* he was necessarily delineated as lazy, dishonest, and despicable—and first impressions die hard. From this unflattering characterization Donald changed into the less obnoxious but still perverse performer of *Orphan's Benefit.* The world still saw Donald only as a bad guy. Here, from printed discourses, is a small sampling of the adjectives used to describe his nature: *pugnacious, malicious, hostile, frustrated, choleric, splenetic, mercuric, awkward, strident, hammy, ferocious, mean, cranky, cantankerous, fierce.*

As a supporting player (and to diminishing extents as a co-star and star), Donald's most prominent trait was his explosive temper—a wide-ranging expression that went from sputtering rages to passionate screaming to towering tantrums. The least little annoyance or criticism could send him into extended fits of inarticulate quacking. As explored in the 1938 cartoon *Self-Control,* the Duck demonstrated a notable lack of it; he was irascible and thoroughly unapologetic.

Donald was short in stature, but notoriously belligerent. His early animators must have quickly learned how to portray him with raised fists. The Duck would unfailingly challenge anyone and everyone who dared to cross him—from an enormous eagle in *Alpine Climbers* and uncomprehending automatons of *Modern Inventions* in the thirties, to the tiny chipmunks Chip and Dale in the fifties. At other times he was cocky, self-centered, and undeniably arrogant—but he had such flair that no one could ever dislike him for it.

The truth in this matter was that Donald's glaring negativity had a sneaky way of becoming an asset. He channeled all his anger and anxiety into a determination that was more than admirable—it was positively inspiring. Lesser ducks than Donald would have shuffled off the stage before the brick-slinging little monsters of *Orphan's Benefit.* Many of Mickey's ventures would have failed without the dauntless Duck. But it never occurred to Donald to abandon his boundless determination. If it had, he might have given up, seeing that the odds were always against him. In writing about this "tilting at windmills" stance of Donald's one critic has faulted him for being self-deluded. The case is strong for both points of view.

The other side of the early Donald Duck was his artiness—his sensitivity to music and poetry—a wonderful trait that balanced his coarser aspects. It was originally Ducky Nash's idea to have Donald sing, but it never would have worked if Donald had not had the potential to become a multifaceted personality. His presentations of "Mary Had a Little Lamb" and "Little Boy Blue" and his serenade to Donna Duck in *Don Donald* worked incredibly well within the context of each cartoon. They were integrated into the plot, served to develop the character, and provided moments of dazzling high comedy.

And as quickly as Donald's essential character was being established, the critics were making heroic attempts to get to the bottom of his mysterious attraction. Like other artists who had profound meanings read into their work, the animators at the studio found these analyses a constant source of amusement. But to Disney himself it was no laughing matter. Near the end of his life, he would tell of a related horror: "I've always had a nightmare. I dream that one of my pictures has ended up in an art theater. And I wake up shaking."

It can be assumed, then, that the in-depth profiles of Donald, and to a lesser degree other characters, must have at least caused some small shivers to run down Disney's spine. But like it or not, he and his menagerie were often in the pages of national and special interest publications. Following are some of the "chillers."

In July 1939, *Living Age* (the weekly organ of the British Broadcasting Corporation) looked at Donald and concluded in a calm and intellectual assessment that it was his very "duckness" that made him so irresistible. Writing with appropriate British reserve (compare it to the American critic who gushed, "I'm stuck on Donald Duck!"), the author takes the view that some things, people, and objects are naturally funny and laughter-provoking, and it is Donald's very identity as a duck that turns him into such a successful comedian. "It is not from any action they take, any coherent sequence of ideas to which they give rise. . .[that] *Ducks are funny, swans are not;* that seems to have been accepted as axiomatic ever since man first made graphic records of his reaction to the world around him." As further evidence of this view, the writer cites poet F. W. Harvey's lines: "From the troubles of the world/I turn to ducks,/Beautiful comical things. . . ."

The philosopher Henri Bergson would have disagreed with this BBC writer. In his famous essay "Laughter," he states that animals, by their very nature, are *not* funny. We laugh only because we detect some human attitude or expression in them.

The same article then goes on to examine another important aspect of Donald's animal magnetism ("That Donald is worth looking at is likely to be accepted *nemine contradicente*, [without contradiction]" it had imperiously pronounced in the beginning). The BBC had noted that broadcasts of Silly Symphonies had proved surprisingly successful over the airwaves, and thus the writer came to the conclusion that when all was said and done it was Donald's voice that held the magic. "Even when divorced from the gay and startling antics with which he is so skilled at delighting our eyes, it appears that the voice of Donald, a modern echo of the *brekekkekex, co-ax, co-ax* of *The Frogs* [by Aristophanes], falls pleasantly upon our ear. For the fact is that Donald makes good broadcasting."

Yes, Donald made good broadcasting, but he made

infinitely better viewing. No matter how funny his garbled voice was in itself, his humor was by no means totally verbal. Although he occasionally hurled an insult or spit out a nasty comment, Donald was not known for his biting remarks or brilliant sarcasm. Rather, his voice served to enhance a total comedic appeal—one that went far beyond mere words.

On the screen Donald was able to use the full range of his personality and the full complement of his talents. Sometimes to draw laughs he had only to shake a tailfeather or flash his malevolent grin. The gags in Donald's cartoons always worked so well because they evolved as a natural extension of his personality. Donald was one comedian who wouldn't do *anything* for a laugh; it had to be in character.

Naturally, we are not consciously aware of any of this when we snicker at Donald's practical jokes or roar as he gets his comeuppance. Nor is such understanding crucial to our pleasure in him. Still, philosophers, scholars, teachers, and scientists have tried to explain the subconscious effects Donald has on adults and children. Their observations should not be totally ignored; they are good arguments for reintroducing Donald into today's movie theaters.

One teacher has likened Donald to the hero of a moral fable. "When we see our whims and petty vices in animal form, as in Donald Duck, they are funny, and once recognized, we have already taken the first step toward their correction."

Some years later a London child psychologist concluded from a study of seven-to fifteen-year-olds that it is the character of Donald Duck that pleases youngsters. The Duck's response to his own world is much like their own—honest, unrepressed, selfish—and his character is constant—a great psychological comfort to children accustomed to the unpredictability of real adults. Still another enticement to children is vicarious participation in Donald's madcap adventures. Surely a more exciting companion cannot be found—at least, among those they are allowed to play with.

But what explains the hordes of grown-up Duck lovers?

Interestingly enough, the same things about Donald that appeal to children strike a nerve in adults, except that we are experiencing them from a different perspective. For instance, instead of identifying with such Donald-esque responses as hitting a tormentor or ranting and raving at an authority figure, we are envious, knowing we do not act that way. Still, we long to shed the inhibitions that we feel growing up and civilization have forced upon us. More simply, we're dying to tell people what we really think!

An adult, too, can readily identify with Donald's troubles. We feel the frustration, the anger, the burning humiliations—yet remain detached enough to laugh because it is happening on the screen, not in our lives. The result is that we come out of a

Donald's coat of arms reflects his family's continuing tradition of frustration and exasperation.

Donald Duck cartoon feeling relieved, smug, and maybe even superior. With entertainment that boosts morale so well, what adult could not like Donald Duck?*

A more complex observation is on record from Viana Moog, a Brazilian educator and lecturer. Most Donald Duck fans will probably take exception to her theory. She includes Donald Duck in "Symbols of Our Times," typecasting him as one of life's flagrant losers:

As a conception, Donald Duck is Walt Disney's most prodigious creation. Donald is absolutely original and an exclusive product of our epoch. He is the ideal representative of that class of people whom fate condemns to go through life in a perpetual flurry of effort, self-delusion and constant grumbling. Nothing is more odious to Donald than to live in obscurity. Never will he accept a secondary role in life. But the poor fellow has no talent for success, except in the realm of the ridiculous. He has neither beauty, dignity nor respectability. He was not born to be a hero. He poses for tragedy and everything he attempts ends in comedy.

Still another theory of Donald's personality is that he is the product of the Depression—that in the face of economic adversity, he had to be born tough, stubborn, and crafty. It seems only inevitable that the point should have been made forty years ago, but odds are that Donald would have been the same no matter what the era. The fact was that Disney sorely needed his "bad boy."

This tiny sampling of what has been written about Donald illustrates that perhaps no other animated character has such a rich potential for analysis (it's a wonder that *he* didn't wind up on Sigmund Frump's couch in *Donald's Dilemma* instead of Daisy!). But sometimes the theorizing, however tongue-in-cheek, did get out of hand. A perfect example comes from a 1938 *New York Times* editorial penned on the occasion of Disney's honorary M.A. from Harvard. It described his whole screen output as "a free interpretation of life on campus, one long parable of collegiate animation." In it, Mickey was The Eternal Freshman; the Big Bad Wolf, the World Outside; Snow White, Truth; the Dwarfs, Alumni. And how did Donald Duck fit into the picture? "Testy Donald Duck, as the name implies, is obviously the typical college don."

It is easy to understand why Disney had nightmares.

And while the world was trying so hard to unravel Donald's mystery, behind the gates of the Studio the Duck was being groomed for his fast-approaching stardom. Walt was quick to have his fine feathered friend join Mickey in the "endorsement" business so successfully established by Kay Kamen. In a short time, Donald's early character merchandise was worn, carried, eaten, drunk, played with, washed with, and even sneezed into by Duck lovers from coast to coast.

*Answer: The contrary ex-Beatle Ringo Starr. In a 1963 fan magazine he revealed his only dislikes as onions and Donald Duck!

Merchandise: Duckmania

Although the Donald Duck watch never acquired quite the cachet of the Mickey timepiece, Duck merchandise has been popular and collectible since the first piece was manufactured in the 1930s. Over the years, Donald turned up as toys in all shapes and sizes, on clothes, bed linens, china, and even on foods—Donald Duck Succotash, for example. The following represent just a fraction of the items made in the last forty years. Of them, some can still be found in flea markets and secondhand shops; the most sought-after pieces can be acquired through collectors and at auctions.

Left: An early Donald Duck doll.
Below: A Donald Duck rubber ball.

Mechanical Donald toys that roll, hop, and whirl.

Donald's wink was prominent on much of his early merchandise.

Donald Duck cookie jars manufactured in the thirties and forties have become collector's items today.

A Donald Duck train car from the 1930s.

Co-Star

With Donald so easily stealing the show in his first two appearances, there was nothing left for Disney to do but give the public what it wanted. However, still unsure whether Donald would prove an enduring performer or just another momentary flicker in the Hollywood galaxy of stars, Disney decided to build up Donald slowly but surely. He let him appear in a number of Mickey Mouse cartoons—the greatest honor around the Studio—beginning with *The Dognapper,* which shortly followed *Orphan's Benefit* in 1934.

In the three-year period during which he officially functioned as a co-star, Donald Duck started on his steady course of character improvement by developing an amazing versatility that easily equaled Mickey's. No longer confined to his role as a mere pest, Donald entered new situations that brought out his more positive aspects; he went from garage mechanic to fireman to whaler to South Seas ukulele player without ever losing any of the wonderfully unredeeming qualities that made the nation love him so passionately.

During this time, too, he underwent a physical transformation that rid him of his ugly, gawky look. Donald Duck expert

Jack Hannah explains that the change was not a cold and calculated move on the part of the animators. Rather, it was a natural progression according to the way they perceived the Duck. As the artists got to know and understand Donald's character better, the stories they were writing suggested another look. Donald's rounder figure and cuteness conveyed a character with a less grim and disagreeable first impression, one with more dimension and more charisma. His newly gained good looks also functioned to mask his true personality, making his bad behavior and tantrums more surprising and ultimately funnier when they surfaced.

Of all Donald's co-starring roles, one of his earliest was certainly his greatest. *The Band Concert*, released in 1935, was Mickey Mouse's first appearance in Technicolor (all the better to see the Mouse turn livid at Donald!), and in it Donald played his favorite role—that of the malicious adversary.

The scene of the concert is outdoors in a park. Just as Maestro Mickey is about to start the *William Tell Overture*, Donald Duck appears as a noisy vendor distracting both the

Above and opposite: **Donald's impertinent flute solo in *The Band Concert* (1935) both enraged Maestro Mickey and upstaged him. Another maestro, Arturo Toscanini, was dazzled by the Duck's virtuoso performance. He was reported to have seen *The Band Concert* six times.**

In *The Band Concert*, Donald hawks peanuts and ice cream before reaching into his sleeve for his unending supply of magic flutes. The first Mickey Mouse cartoon in color, it gave Donald his most memorable and acclaimed role as co-star.

audience and Mickey with his loud cries for peanuts, popcorn, and ice cream, and with his unasked-for addition to the program—an impertinent flute rendition of "Turkey in the Straw." From that point on, all-out war breaks loose between Mickey and Donald as Mickey keeps smashing Donald's flute and Donald keeps pulling new ones from his sleeve. The wit, imagination, and technical skill of its creators turned this confrontation into one of the most memorable battles in animation history. Critics were effusive in their praise, especially Gilbert Seldes, writing in *Esquire*:

The Band Concert is Disney's greatest single work and I doubt very much whether half a dozen works produced in America at the same time in all other arts can stand comparison with this one. What Mr. Henry James might have called the "dazzling, damning apparation" of Donald Duck in this picture is only a small part of its glory. I know of no other Mickey Mouse in which all the elements are so miraculously blended. It has comedy of detail—such as the sleeve of Mickey's oversized uniform continually slipping down to conceal his baton; it has comedy of structure based on the duck's persistent attempts to break up the concert by playing a competing tune on the flute; it has comedy of character in the stern artistic devotion of Mickey contrasted with the unmotivated villainy of Donald... the total effect is miraculous....

As a comedy team, Mickey and Donald were outstanding. When they got together on screen, either one of two scenarios developed: Mickey's goodness acted as a foil for Donald's evil (as in *The Band Concert*) or Mickey acted as a straightman to Donald's solo antics (as in *Orphans' Benefit* and *Mickey's Circus*). Together the Mouse and the Duck acted out unforgettable scenes of anger, frustration, dismay, surprise, confusion, and rivalry, and played out scores of side-splitting gags. Donald, always more of a ham, got the bigger laughs.

In his subsequent appearances with Mickey and Goofy, Donald was part of a spirited team often bound for high adventure. In the midst of each cartoon he always managed to have his own crises (one angry outburst per film was *de rigueur*) before joining the others in what was usually a happy ending. *Alpine Climbers* has him battling a rambunctious mountain goat and a fearsome eagle before returning to save Mickey from a fall and Pluto from the ministrations of a well-meaning St. Bernard. Donald took part similarly in *Moose Hunters* and in tamer adventures such as *Mickey's Polo Team* and *Hawaiian Holiday*.

Another favorite role for the Duck as co-star was "problem solver." The comic possibilities in that realm were endless for Donald, since he inevitably made things worse just by being there. And on top of that, he could get good and mad when things went wrong! The setting for these types of hazards were usually occupational. For instance, in *Mickey's Service Station* he totally destroys a car in search of a squeak that turns out to be a cricket's chirp; in *Donald and Pluto,* he is a frustrated plumber trying to fix a pipe while Pluto, having swallowed a magnet, is attracting nothing but trouble; and in *Mickey's Fire Brigade,* the Duck heats up the action when he comes to the

Having attracted a bull moose by dressing as a sexy decoy, an uncostumed Donald now flees his disappointed—and angry—quarry. *Moose Hunters* (1937), an adventure/comedy, was typical of Donald's and Mickey's co-starring exploits.

Ghost exterminating was one of the co-stars' more unusual occupations in *Lonesome Ghosts* (1937).

In *Hawaiian Holiday* (1937), Minnie danced the hula to the lilting strains of Mickey's guitar and Donald's ukulele.

rescue of a dressmaker's dummy. Obviously Donald was always better *as* a problem than *at* one.

At still other times Donald joined Mickey and Goofy to face a common foe. In structure these episodes were similar to the adventure stories, with the exception that a tangible evil took the place of the challenge provided by a mountain or building a boat. Since any friend of Mickey's was a friend of Donald's, it followed that any enemy would be hostile to the Duck, too. Thus, Donald found himself in direct opposition to the brutal Pegleg Pete, who was getting around on two good legs by the mid-thirties (earlier, he had sported one wooden leg) and was as terrifying as ever. In *Moving Day,* for instance, Pete is a heartless sheriff who serves a trembling Donald and Mickey with an eviction notice. He also inspired fear and loathing as the vicious *Dognapper,* and in later years as the equally vicious *New Neighbor.* A 1937 cartoon, *Lonesome Ghosts,* had the terrific trio up against a supernatural foe. As "ghost exterminators" Donald, Mickey, and Goofy wage a bumbling attack against resident poltergeists, who finally flee when they mistake our flour-covered heroes for rival ghosts.

In all, the Donald-Mickey-Goofy team was extremely successful, if short-lived. Donald's last appearance in a Mickey Mouse cartoon was in 1942's *Symphony Hour,* and he gave his final film performance with his co-stars in the "Mickey and the Beanstalk" segment of the feature *Fun and Fancy Free* in 1947. By 1937, Donald's story crew was confident that the Duck had enough dramatic potential to sustain a plot on his own. That

Fun and Fancy Free (1947) was one of the few full-length films to feature Donald, Mickey, and Goofy. In the Happy Valley sequence (also known as "Mickey and the Beanstalk") narrated by Edgar Bergen and Charlie McCarthy, a starving Donald and Goofy season their meager meal with salty tears.

year Walt gave the go-ahead for Donald's top billing. Mickey Mouse was no longer the only Disney character to have his own cartoons.

In fact the move made Donald unique in animation history. Seldom did a cartoon character make such a remarkable career progression, even though the phenomenon of the rising star was common enough in live-action films. Since the beginning of animated cartoons, characters—including Krazy Kat, Felix the Cat, Flip the Frog, Betty Boop, and Popeye—had come to the screen as full-fledged principals to succeed or fail without the benefit of film tryouts. (Sometimes, as was the case with Popeye and Krazy Kat, the character had first proved himself in a comic strip.) Those who did start out in supporting roles—Olive Oyl, Bluto, or Ignatz Mouse, for example—never had the strength or appeal to make star status. If we translate this into television terms, Donald Duck was one of the few characters who became a "spin-off"—and, as happens on TV so infrequently, his series became more popular and enduring than the original.

Opposite: **Donald and Goofy sing for their supper to no avail just before selling their cow for some magic beans.**

Below: **Goofy and Mickey corral the hunger-crazed Donald.**

Mickey's Fire Brigade (1935). **The heroes to the rescue of Clarabelle!**

Mickey, it seems, winds up sitting down on the job, while Donald, as usual, has an ax to grind.

In a scene from *Mickey's Polo Team* (1936) Donald follows Mickey into the fray.

Mickey's Grand Opera (1936) finds Donald in fine voice . . . until he literally gets a frog in his throat.

On *Moving Day* (1936), Donald gathers his worldly possessions—pots, pans, rakes, a lamp, a bird, and a fish.

Donald's love of performing led him to *Mickey's Amateurs* in 1937.

Magician Mickey (1937). Playing the familiar role of pest, Donald pulls a rabbit out of his sailor hat to heckle Mickey.

When the Duck finally comes on stage, his shenanigans cause a near riot.

In *Boat Builders* (1938), the co-stars set sail in a folding boat.

Mickey and Goofy are dumbfounded when the vessel sinks, but Donald has words befitting a sailor.

The Making of
a Donald Duck
Cartoon

Every Donald Duck cartoon began with rough pencil sketches.

Opposite: "I've always wanted a good camera," said Walt Disney. He finally got the best when the Disney Studio developed the multiplane camera, which revolutionized animation.

Of all the remarks that have been made about Walt Disney, one of the most often quoted comes from the great English political cartoonist David Low. He called Disney "the most significant figure in graphic art since Leonardo"—despite the fact that Disney himself never aspired to "art" and preferred to consider himself an entertainer for the masses.

Certainly Disney did much to inspire the comment. He was an enormous talent, a relentless technical innovator and inventor, a man driven by his vision. The intensity of his devotion is even more staggering when one realizes the amount of work that went into a seven-to eight-minute short. To Disney, however, eight minutes or less was time enough to unfold a masterpiece of economy. Many of his masterpieces, like those of Leonardo, are now important parts of museum collections all over the world.

What set Disney's cartoons so far apart from all the others of the era was their superiority in both technique and content. Nearly every advance that was made in the field of animation came out of the Disney Studio, including the perfection of Technicolor, sophisticated synchronization methods, and—perhaps the biggest advance of all—the multiplane camera. Developed within the Studio over a number of years, this special piece of apparatus made it possible to give animated film a realistic three-dimensional effect without the usual hazard of size distortion. That is, background and foreground art could remain in their proper perspectives as the human eye would see them when the camera moved in or pulled back from a scene. In addition, the multiplane allowed the creation of special effects previously unattainable with conventional cameras—expressive blurs in action, glows radiating from objects, splashes and ripples in water—all of which made cartoons more spectacular than ever. For this invention alone, in 1937, the Motion Picture Academy gave Disney a special award for scientific achievement. *The Old Mill* (1937) was the first short made using the multiplane camera.

It was never enough for Disney to dazzle audiences with wonderful effects and catchy music—there had to be substance

Serious work at the Disney Studio. This scene typifies the story men at work.

Opposite, above: Donald and Daisy fresh from the inkers and ready for the color department.

Opposite, below: The Disney model sheets were extremely detailed and enabled animators to give Donald a consistent look.

behind the fireworks, the tale had to be entertaining in itself, and there had to be "Disney dust" (the showers of sparkles that became his trademark). Although Walt never had formal training in developing stories, he had marvelous ideas and intuition for plot, gags, and pacing. He and his animators also studied the great silent film comedies to learn about such things as camera angles and editing, but the basic ideas came from Disney and his well-chosen staff. Over the years it included such talented men as Ub Iwerks, Fred Spencer, Art Babbitt, Paul Allen, Johnny Cannon, Jack King, Carl Barks, and especially, when it came to Donald Duck, Jack Hannah.

In 1933, Hannah was a 20-year-old poster designer from San Diego looking for commercial artwork during the depth of the Depression. Like Ducky Nash, he was urged to go to the Disney Studio, although he had no particular desire to be a cartoonist. Hannah left his portfolio there and soon got a call. As he likes to tell it, he then reported for "a two-week tryout that lasted thirty years." In that time he came to be an important and respected member of the Disney crew.

Hannah first brought his outrageous imagination to the Duck as an animator on *Modern Inventions.* He continued to work on Donald—at one point he teamed with Carl Barks in the story department—right through the television years.

Eighteen of the cartoons he directed were honored with Oscar nominations. Of all the Duck stories, Hannah's have been praised as the wildest. They include such memorable cartoons as *Don Donald*, *Self-Control*, *Donald Gets Drafted*, *Chip 'n' Dale*, *Double Dribble* (in which basketball players sported the names of animators), and many episodes on the Disney TV show. No one else but Hannah could have made Donald such a lovable terror.

Words alone cannot do justice to the content of a Donald Duck cartoon. They fail to convey the effect of one of Donald's demon rages or the utter flamboyance when he flirts: "Hiya toots!" Words *can* convey the process and complexity of how those powerful scenes were brought to the screen. Before we proceed with Donald's life, then, we must know about the making of one of his cartoons.

One might imagine that to create all the mirth and merriment that were so characteristic of a Disney cartoon, the Studio was filled with happy workers whistling and singing like the Seven Dwarfs. It's been said that at times the workrooms did take on such an atmosphere, and at others the feeling of a college fraternity house. However it seemed to the outsider, there was always serious business going on. The creation of a Disney short was a highly technical matter ultimately depending on science and mathematics. Surprisingly cold and calculating, perhaps, but it was the basis of Disney's art.

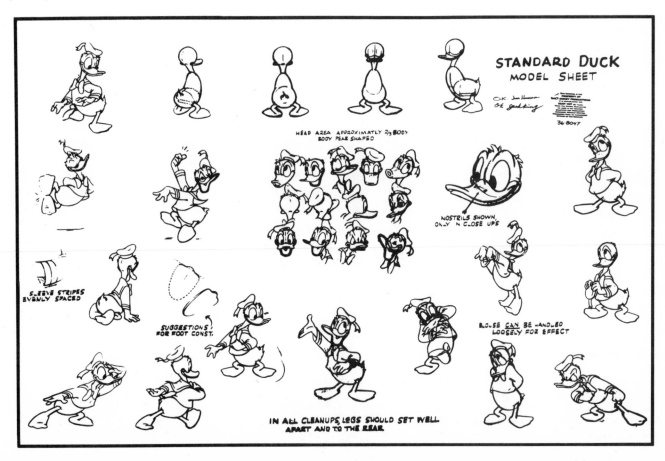

Storyboard sketches indicated action and dialogue. In actual production, the sound track was recorded before any drawing was made.

Opposite: An animated cartoon has no script, but is done with the aid of storyboards and drafts. This draft from *Donald's Nephews* shows how each scene was listed by animator and included the footage completed. *S* stands for still; *P* for pan (or panorama); *CU* for close-up; *LS* for long shot; and *MCU* for medium close-up.

To understand how the cartoons were made, it is first helpful to know about the overall structure and setup of the Studio. After the boon of the 1930s Disney moved to fifty-one acres on a lot in Burbank (its present site) and employed over four-hundred people in a myriad of specializations. All of them were needed for the making of a single cartoon. A fifty-page organization memo put into effect in 1938 reflected the increased intricacy of cartoon making since the days when everything was done by Walt, Roy, and a few others. Among the titles for which responsibilities and duties were described were: production supervisor, technical research director, department head, unit supervisor, head layout man, color model director, background supervisor, promotion and story research supervisor, effects-in-between department manager, and scores of others. Luckily, there was also a coordinating department, although no one was better at coordinating everything—from conception to the international marketing of a cartoon—than Walt himself.

Preproduction

The ideas for Disney's cartoons were first suggested to him by a staff hired to be "idea" men. They were then submitted to the story department, soon after which a story conference was held. At these highly creative sessions, attended by the musical directors as well as Walt and the story men, the plot and its gags were outlined and visualized practically frame by frame. At the end of these hour to hour-and-a-half sessions, there would be scores of sketches pinned to a wall, comprising what was known as the "storyboard." From this progression of rough drawings Disney could tell exactly how the entire cartoon would run on the screen. (In fact, this technique proved so successful that it was later used to design the live-action films. Disney credited its invention to Webb Smith, an animator who had been a newspaper cartoonist.) The storyboard was then turned over to the cartoon director, at which point the mathematics of animation entered the picture.

Every step in Disney animation was based on two constants of 35mm film: that there were sixteen frames to the foot of film and twenty-four frames to the second. Thus, if a cartoon was to run for seven minutes, the director knew that the length would be 630 feet. It was then easy to divide the entire length by the number of scenes in order to allot the number of feet and frames for each individual scene. Similarly, it was just as easy to calculate that over 10,000 frames—each done by hand and taking from one to several hours to complete—would be needed for the entire picture.

The Sound Track

Once the calculations were made, the director prepared a work sheet listing the animators, footage each was assigned, and descriptions of action and sound in each scene.

SEQ. NO.		SEQ. TITLE			
DIRECTOR			ASST. DIR.	LAYOUT MAN	SEC'Y

SCENE No.	ARTIST	SCREEN FOOTAGE	B. G. DATA	DESCRIPTION OF ACTION
1	QUACKENBUSH	28-12 Anim. Scr.	S	CU - Postcard - Donald turns it over.
2	TOWSLEY	11-02 Anim. Scr.	S	Don hears bell.
3	WILLIAMS	13-12 Anim. Scr.& Efx.	P	Donald opens front door - kids enter - knock Donald up against wall.
4	LOVE	10-0 Anim. Scr.	P	MLS - Kids on bike ride on piano.
5	"	6-06 Anim. Scr.	P	MLS - Kids on bike skid to a stop.
7	TOWSLEY	2-10 Anim. Scr.	P	CU - Donald in milk, pleasant take.
8	LOVE	5-09 Anim. S&¼	S	MCU - Kids laugh - say, "I'M HUEY -- I'M DEWEY -- I'M LOUIE".
9	TOWSLEY	4-13 Anim. Scr.	SA 6	CU - Don says, "HY, HELLO BOYS".
9A	"	3-0 Anim. Scr.	S.	LS - Kids beam - kid reaches for whistle.
10	LOVE	9-4 Anim. Scr.	S	CU - Kid puts whistle in bouth and blows.

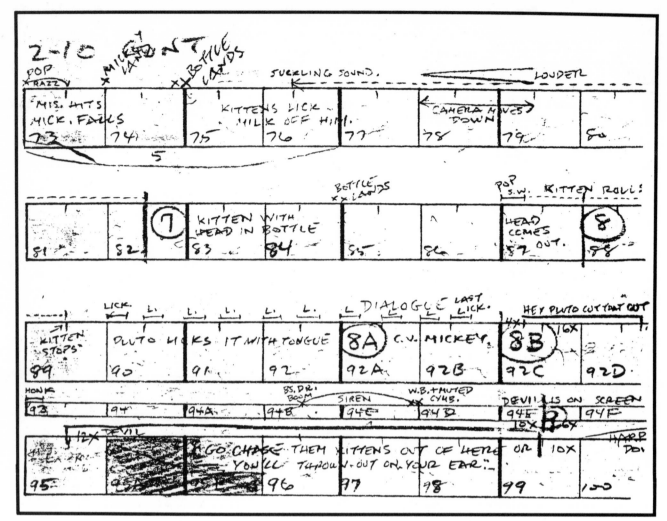

A detail from a bar sheet used to coordinate music and animation.

Production of an animated film began in the sound department. The entire sound track had to be recorded before a single drawing could be attempted. For the purposes of clarity, each type of sound was first mapped out on a complex multiple-staved chart called a "bar sheet"—a diagram that looked like and served the same purpose as a conductor's score. Just by looking at it, musicians and animators could tell exactly (to the foot) where each sound accent would fall on the film and get an overview of the sound in relation to the action.

For each cartoon, three separate tracks—dialogue, sound-effects, and music—were recorded. Of the three, the dialogue was most critical to the action, for it determined the pacing. Before an animator could draw Donald saying hello, for instance, he had to know how many frames it would take. The sound man would record the word and time it and then provide the animator with the necessary information.

Less crucial but still important to the visuals was the sound-effects track. The "noise men" knew exactly where they had to insert their crashes, whistles, slams, and crunches. The methods they used to produce their effects were nothing less than ingenious—from a derby hat rapidly poked with a finger for a motorboat to the rubbing of a sandy palm close to the microphone for a giant eating celery.

The music, too, had its own special recording requirements throughout the cartoon. It was governed by a tempo known as "six time," meaning that there was a beat every six frames. As the musicians recorded their score, they listened to a metronome through earphones to reinforce their timing. Their achievements in this area turned out to be quite formidable, as noted by the famous composer Jerome Kern. He wrote in the New York *Journal* on May 25, 1936: "Cartoonist Walt Disney has made the twentieth century's only important contribution to music. Disney has made use of music as language. In the synchronization of humorous episodes with humorous music, he has unquestionably given us the outstanding contribution of our time...the only real contribution."

When all of the tracks were individually laid down and approved—as everything else was—by Disney, they were then combined onto one track to await their final merger with the film. Although there were still no drawings at this point, the beauty of mathematics proved itself again and again. When sound and action were brought together the first time, they *always* matched perfectly.

Huey gets a knuckle sandwich, but it's Donald who's in pain in this rough sketch for Donald's Nephews.

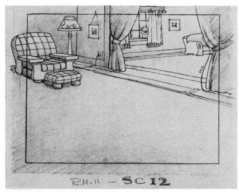

A detail from a background painting of Donald's living room.

Background paintings in animation remain constant, but the characters, shot against this background, move within the frame.

Animation

With the sound completed, the animators could begin their work. Head animators took their cues from the mathematical instructions established by the sound department and proceeded to create the extremes of movement in sequence. If Donald had sixteen frames in which to fall on his face, the head animator would draw frames 1, 8, and 16. It was up to an assistant known as an "in-betweener" to fill in the action of the other frames, and then to yet another assistant to do the details and shading. While the characters were drawn one to a page in this manner, another set of artists did the background art. The reason for this division of labor was to fit the artist to his expertise, temperament, or particular flair for a certain character. It would have been foolish to stifle a highly creative mind by assigning him to details and shading, just as it would have been wasteful to put a good Duck man on Goofy. And, according to Jack Hannah, many of Disney's animators were unsuccessful with the Duck. Not everyone, as he did, could throw himself into such a crazy character.

The next step in a cartoon's production was to take the animators' pencil sketches and photograph the film in the rough. At this stage again, it was subject to Disney's intense scrutiny. After his approval, the sketches were "cleaned up" and transferred to celluloid—clear sheets of plastic called "cels" for short. This step was the only job in the Studio that was handled entirely by women. One story had it that their smaller hands were best suited to the delicate work.

When they received the sketches, the women in the inking department placed a piece of celluloid over the 9½-inch by 12½-

Detailed Duck Cleanup

SHADED PART COMPLETELY ENCLOSED ONLY WHEN EYE SHADOW OR HI-LITES ARE CALLED FOR··

OTHERWISE A SIMPLE SUGGESTION OF ROUNDNESS IS SUFFICIENT····

··DON'S BILL··
NORMAL OR DISTORTED, IT SHOULD ALWAYS BE CLEARLY OUTLINED TO DISTINGUISH IT FROM THE DIFFERENTLY COLORED HEAD AND NECK OR INSIDE OF BILL·····

Donald's bill proved especially expressive to animators.

inch sketch and traced the outlines in India ink. In the late 1950s this time-consuming step was replaced by a Xerox photography process developed by Ub Iwerks. The camera photographed the original pencil sketches and the black outlines appeared on celluloid.

After hundreds of preliminary paintings were done to determine the most pleasing combinations, an opaque color was applied to the other side of the cel. In this case, the painting was a process that demanded much more than even brush-strokes. Frank Daugherty described Disney's "wonderful world of color" in 1940, revealing the unique problems of Technicolor and, as always, Disney's quest for perfection:

A Disney color chart of course would just about take the water colorists' breath away.... He utilizes, for example, some 2,000 or more different shades and colors, all expertly catalogued by number, not by name, so that the many girls in his inking and painting department can reach out and get the right bottle immediately...colors on the screen in the Technicolor process are never the same as the colors you start out with when you begin to paint them on celluloid. In the Disney process, the workers work on five or six layers of celluloid, superimposing

Women did most of the inking and painting in the 1930s and '40s.

Opposite: In a scene from *The Reluctant Dragon*, Robert Benchley visits the camera room, where Old MacDonald Duck springs to life.

one color over another, and this causes a constant change of original colors which has to be compensated for before the paint is applied [Also, the color is magnified some four-hundred times when it reaches the screen].... Of course, this hasn't been done all at once. The Disney artists are still learning. They know, for example, that purples and dark green and dark blues and most other dark colors nearly always go black when shown on the screen...it is impossible to apply a dark brown without streaking it...the greatest studio discovery they think has been in the simple matter of getting a blue that can be used for background, against which other paints will not go brown or black. They have achieved this with an imported monastral blue, very expensive, but worth all they pay for it.... The Disney people can't guess...they have to know.

Looking at the other side of color was film historian Lewis Jacobs, who focused on the creative aspect of Disney's use of color and hailed his imagination:

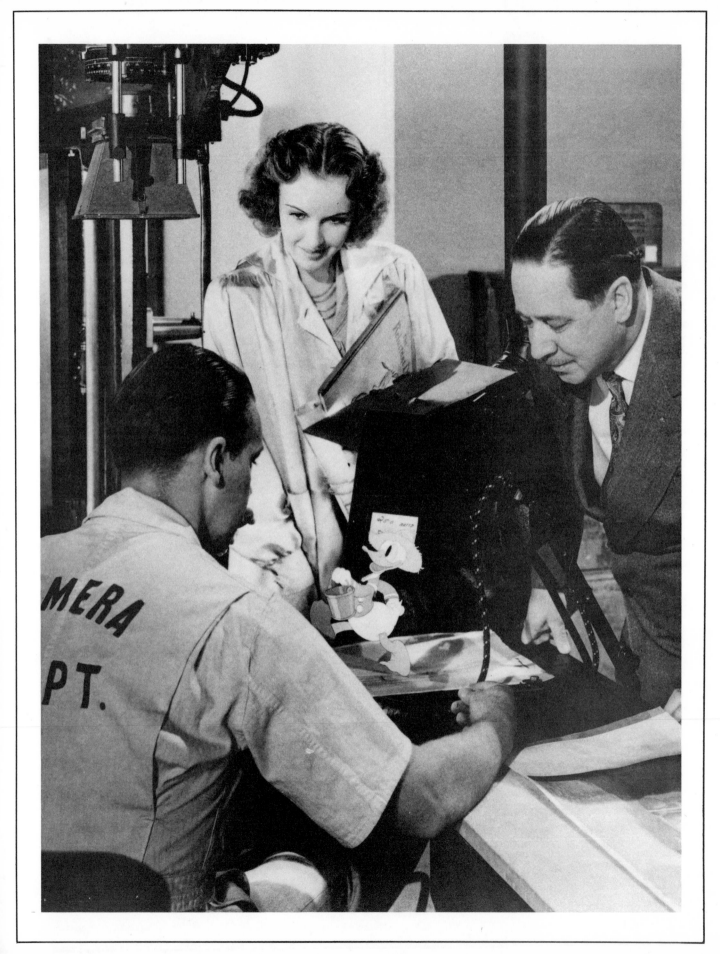

Walt looks on as one of his story men presents his latest brainstorm. The storyboard was one of the many Disney innovations in animation. It was so successful as a technique that it is still in use today for both animated and live-action films.

Disney was the first to realize that color in motion pictures need not bear any resemblance to color in real life, that objects on the screen could be endowed with any pigmentation dictated by the imagination. Furthermore, he recognized that color on screen need not be static, but could move, and that such mobility, affecting the emotions, produced new visual experiences . . . when the wolf tried to blow down the house of the three pigs, he literally blew himself blue in the face; when the north wind swept through an autumn forest, the entire color scheme changed from golden red to icy blue . . . .

If the color proved perfect, a final production sheet was issued and the cels were sent to the camera department. There the necessary characters for each frame were positioned against the appropriate background painting on a specially lighted table. The cameraman photographed the cel and then repeated the process with 10,000 more cels. With a method as

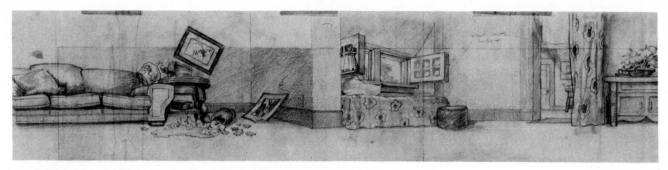

complicated, exacting, and time-consuming as this, it is understandable that Disney's cartoons were very expensive. And adding to the expense was the producer's penchant to throw out footage and reshoot at any cost whenever he detected the least little flaw.

In 1935 it was reported that the average cost of a Disney short was about $35,000. Richard Schickel, in *The Disney Version*, gives a complete breakdown of the costs as follows: $27,500 for production, $17,500 for prints, $5,000 for advertising, shipping, taxes, and miscellaneous costs, bringing the total expense to $50,000. (Today the same seven-minute film would cost ten to fifteen times as much.) After eighteen months, if the short was successful, the Studio would get the money back. Disney always plowed this money right back into his next projects and, as costs spiraled, looked for ways to cut back. He found them with little problem.

The most obvious cost savers can be seen in the films themselves. For all those who have always wondered why Donald (and Mickey) only have four fingers, economy is the answer. Without the extra digit, animators saved precious time as well as thousands of dollars. For the same reason, Disney cartoons contain few crowd scenes, no elaborate costume extravaganzas, and always show lions on the prowl instead of tigers (no stripes to animate!). In contrast, economy was *not* the reason for Donald's much-criticized habit of not wearing pants. Disney thought the Duck's bottom was wonderfully expressive —why cover it up?

In all, the making of a Donald Duck cartoon was a painstaking and difficult business. And even when the film was finished, Disney was still not content to leave his work alone. As part of his constant effort to top himself, he demanded honest feedback from his people. Mandatory postproduction screenings were not held just for pleasure—written critiques were required from everyone.

With such meticulous attention, such high standards, and such unflagging determination from so many great talents, the Disney Studio was able to assume its unchallenged position as the leader in animation. On pages 81–93 we present *Donald's Nephews*, one of the most popular of Donald Duck's many early classics.

A rough sketch from *Donald's Nephews* shows Donald doing a slow burn.

> "We thought we were always going to be twenty-one years old. We thought we would always be putting goldfish in the bottled drinking water, balancing cups of water on the light fixtures, changing the labels on cans of sauerkraut juice. We were twenty-one years old, Walt was thirty, leading the pack. Working there was more fun than any job I could ever imagine."
>
> —Ward Kimball

Back to the Drawing Board

In the early days at Disney, visitors touring the Studio would bring back reports of employees who were seen grimacing, grinning, mugging for each other, wildly gesticulating, emitting weird sounds, and generally acting like maniacs. These "crazies"—all high-spirited men in their twenties—were none other than the animators, and their fits of lunacy amounted to an exercise in creativity. In choosing and rendering the facial and bodily reactions of their subjects, they were limited only by their imaginations and inhibitions. They were "actors with pencils, and they would risk any loss of dignity to study their lines, as it were," noted Richard Schickel. The animators' creative freedom also extended to a surprising lack of pressure; they were not required to complete a certain amount of footage per day, and Disney even encouraged them to throw out work that did not meet the highest standards.

In their more serene moments of work, the animators used three-dimensional models of their subjects to study organic structure and movement. They also worked from model sheets compiled by head animators, which were filled with handy tips for drawing. Comments on Donald ranged from the wrinkle of his bill in an angry mood to the proper attachment of his feet to an admonition to "watch construction and grouping of hair." Perhaps funniest of all on the model sheets were the samples of Donald in humanly impossible "takes."

In addition to the training provided by model sheets, the newer animators were required to attend evening classes twice a week. At first they studied at Chouinard Art School, but in 1932 Disney set up a school right on the Hyperion Studio premises. Don Graham was the first instructor and was later joined by Phil Dike and James Patrick. The students came from a variety of places. "Demand for animators so exceeds the supply, that Disney sent representatives to interview 1,000 applicants in New York last March," reported a newspaper in 1936.

And Disney *was* serious about training his men. In the early years of the school he spent $100,000 a year on the apprentice program, in which students were given intensive instruction in every aspect of animation including the nontechnical. Once Disney even brought in a noted psychology professor to lecture "the boys" on humor. "We had to give it up," Walt said later, somewhat chagrined. "None of us knew what he was talking about." Apparently the man was an Old World doctor who lived up to the worst stereotype of psychologists. He had started off his incomprehensible lecture declaring, "First, ve must answer 'vot iss a gagk?'"

Despite this unsuccessful experiment, Disney trained animators whose technique and "gagks" were the runaway best in the field. Today all but a few of the original crew have retired or died, but a new generation is being groomed to keep the Disney tradition of excellence in animation alive and flourishing.

Donald's Nephews

Look what's come in the morning mail. It's a postcard from Donald's sister.

She says she's sending his nephews for a visit, and they arrive today.

Their names are Huey, Dewey, and Louie. My, don't they look like angels!

Donald is delighted. How wonderful it will be to hear the patter of little feet.

Suddenly the doorbell rings. "There are the little darlings now," says Donald.

Ever the charming host, the unsuspecting Donald opens the door with a smile.

"Welc . . ." Poor Donald doesn't even get his first word out. The boys storm into the house.

That entrance isn't exactly a prelude to a peaceful afternoon of baby-sitting.

Somehow Donald had the impression that his nephews were a little younger.

Well, boys will be boisterous. They're just a little overexcited.

It occurs to Donald that perhaps they shouldn't be riding their tricycles in the house.

Donald's nephews introduce themselves. "I'm Huey!" "I'm Dewey!" "I'm Louie!" The boys hold their polo mallets at attention.

"Why, hello, boys," replies Donald, thinking that, after all, they are just children.

Donald begins to explain to his nephews that polo isn't an indoor game.

He's rudely interrupted when Louie blows his whistle.

The game is on! Donald's nephews charge from room to room, pedaling furiously.

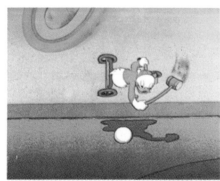

Dewey fields a particularly difficult shot, banking off the wall.

Donald ducks as the ball goes whizzing over his head. Fast game, this polo.

Louie looks around for a goal and whacks the ball back past the hapless Donald.

Too late, Donald realizes where Louie's shot is headed.

Grandma Duck's priceless antique lamp! Oh, no!

The nephews aren't discouraged. Dewey sets up another shot.

Again Donald ducks as all three nephews come pedaling at him.

Oblivious of furniture crashing around him, Huey prepares for another goal.

Bull's-eye!

What a great shot—even if the books did land on the floor.

What's this? *Modern Child Training?* These children could sure use some training.

Let's see . . . musical games! Now that's an idea!

A song would be just the thing to take their little minds off polo.

But in order to play a song, Donald has to make it to the piano.

As he inches his way carefully across the floor, the ball whizzes overhead.

Good! They're in the other room. Carefully, now.

Donald tries a little diversionary tactic to draw the "enemies'" fire.

So far, so good. Very slowly, Donald sets the music up on the stand.

He opens it to "Pop Goes the Weasel." Surely this will work—the book says so.

As he begins to play, Donald watches to see the effect of his strategy.

Louie is the first to skid to a stop. He cocks an ear.

Then Huey and Dewey are attracted by the cheerful tune. Polo is forgotten.

Whew! It's working. There's nothing like a good book!

But Donald's nephews aren't content to sit quietly and listen.

It's Huey on trombone, Dewey on concertina, and Louie on bass!

Suddenly Donald's a conductor. "Now, all together, boys! One, two . . ."

Well, maybe it's not music, but then it's not polo either.

Now it's Dewey on trombone. But he doesn't seem to be paying attention.

An apple from that fruit dish would make a keen mute.

Now he can really blow up a storm—just like Tommy Dorsey.

Donald gets into the spirit and uses his piano like a banjo.

Dewey gets set to wail, but he doesn't know his own strength.

Pop! goes the apple—and *clunk!* goes the piano lid.

Down falls the lid, right on top of poor Uncle Donald!

Donald struggles to free himself and regain his lost dignity.

His nephews collapse in helpless laughter. But their uncle's in no mood to laugh.

In fact, his good nature is starting to wear a little thin.

Then he laughs. It was an honest mistake. Dewey couldn't have done it on purpose.

Or could he? In any case, Donald's willing to try again.

This time it's Louie who has a gleam in his eye—and a bow in his hand.

Intent on the music, Donald doesn't notice that the bass has dropped out of the band.

Louie takes careful aim.

A perfect shot—for everyone but Donald.

Donald grabs the book and is about to throw it at his nephew.

RULE VIII...
Never lose your temper in front of children.

Then the book falls open to a convenient passage.

Donald stops to think. "Yeah, that's right," he agrees.

"Now, boys, you must be nice," Donald admonishes his sheepish nephews.

"Let's go on now." And Donald turns back to his music.

But these three little ducks have more than two tricks up their sleeves.

Like a pitcher checking a runner at first, Donald glances back at them.

Did you ever see such innocent little darlings? They really are angels.

Reassured, Donald turns happily back to playing the piano.

Keeping his uncle off guard, Huey plays his concertina with one foot while he takes careful aim.

Another great shot! All three of these boys are marksmen.

And Donald's their target yet again.

Poor Donald is about to lose his temper again.

"Who did that?" he demands.

Suddenly it's every duck for himself. "Huey did!" "Louie did!" "Dewey did!"

"Who did?" asks Dewey. Forgetting Donald, the boys begin to squabble among themselves.

A hat is knocked off and a punch is thrown.

If those boys keep on this way, Donald's house will be a shambles.

Dismayed by his nephews' behavior, Donald again turns to the book for advice.

He finds that short tempers may mean long appetites.

"Hungry!" muses Donald, relieved to find such a simple solution.

Meanwhile, the boys' argument has degenerated into a brawl.

None too soon, Donald acts to distract his nephews from their quarrel.

"Food! Come and get it!" Donald sings out, confident that this will calm them down.

The boys rush at Donald and grab the turkey out of his hands.

They begin to tear at the roast bird, each trying to get the turkey all to himself.

Donald's not about to stand by and watch his nephews make a mess of the meal.

"Wait a minute!" he commands.
The boys are suddenly quiet. "Sit down!"

As his three nephews take their seats, Donald begins to say grace.

"We give thanks for this food," Donald begins. Then he notices a hand reaching out.

Before Huey can sneak a piece of bread, Donald slaps his hand, then resumes the grace.

"Please make us all good boys," prays Donald, "and bless our happy home. Amen."

The three nephews dive at the turkey as if they'd never had a square meal. Donald is disgusted by their lack of manners.

The boys are fighting over a drumstick, and Donald tries to break it up.

Unfortunately, his hand ends up between two slices of bread.

Huey bites down on his "turkey" sandwich with gusto.

Donald reacts with gusto.

Oh, no! Donald's poor hand is throbbing like a drum.

Now it's swollen to three times its normal size. And does it hurt!

Their Uncle Donald is in pain, and all his nephews can do is laugh.

"This is very exasperating," says Donald, growing very impatient with his nephews' antics.

He turns again to his trusty book for advice—and this time it had better work!

Arouse their sympathy? That should be easy enough, thinks Donald.

Donald replaces the book under his jacket and glances at his nephews.

Then he begins to cry. "Oh, my! I'm so discouraged!" Donald wipes away a tear.

"I've tried so hard!" Donald sobs. "What shall I do? What shall I do?"

Huey, Dewey, and Louie are amazed. "Poor Unca Donald!" remarks Dewey.

They really ought to do something to cheer Donald up. The boys put their heads together.

"We'll be good boys," promises Louie, and he and Huey proceed to fix Donald a piece of pie.

There's no whipped cream for the pumpkin pie, but mustard is a good substitute.

If a little mustard is good, a lot must be even better.

"Here, Unca Donald. Do you want some pie?"

"Pie? And how!" Donald is confident that his strategy has worked.

"That's a nice boy," he praises, giving the contrite little duck a pat on the head. Maybe his nephews aren't as bad as he thought.

"Oh, boy! It worked." Donald congratulates himself as he contemplates the pie.

He opens his beak wide for that first yummy bite . . .

Uh-oh! That was a little too much hot mustard.

"Yeow!"

"Water! Water!" gasps the unfortunate Donald. Huey runs to obey.

But Dewey has anticipated Donald's predicament. He has a bucket ready.

Splash! Dewey drenches Donald. That'll put out the fire.

Of course, what Donald had in mind was a glassful, not a bucketful.

Not satisfied with drowning their uncle, Huey and Louie make up a fire brigade.

But Donald's had enough help. All he wants now is to be left alone.

"Unca Donald!" calls Louie, fire extinguisher at the ready.

Donald yells "Stop!" But the stream of foam bowls him over.

Donald's three nephews decide it's time for their exit. "Good-bye . . ." says Huey.

". . . Unca . . ." Dewey takes his leave after thoughtfully spraying off Donald's face.

". . . Donald!" Louie, the last of the trio, tosses Donald the experts' book. Ouch!

Huey, Dewey, and Louie race off, leaving Donald alone at last in the battered house.

Then Donald happens to glance down at the page of the book that has fallen open.

After all, little children are only angels without wings.

It dawns on Donald that he might have done better without so much "expert" advice.

"Angels without wings? Phooey!" Here's what Donald thinks of the experts.

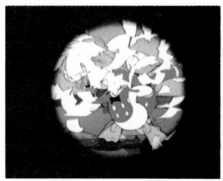

As we fade out, the enraged Donald is burying himself under a flurry of torn pages.

Now, could three little ducklings drive a grown duck berserk? Ask the experts.

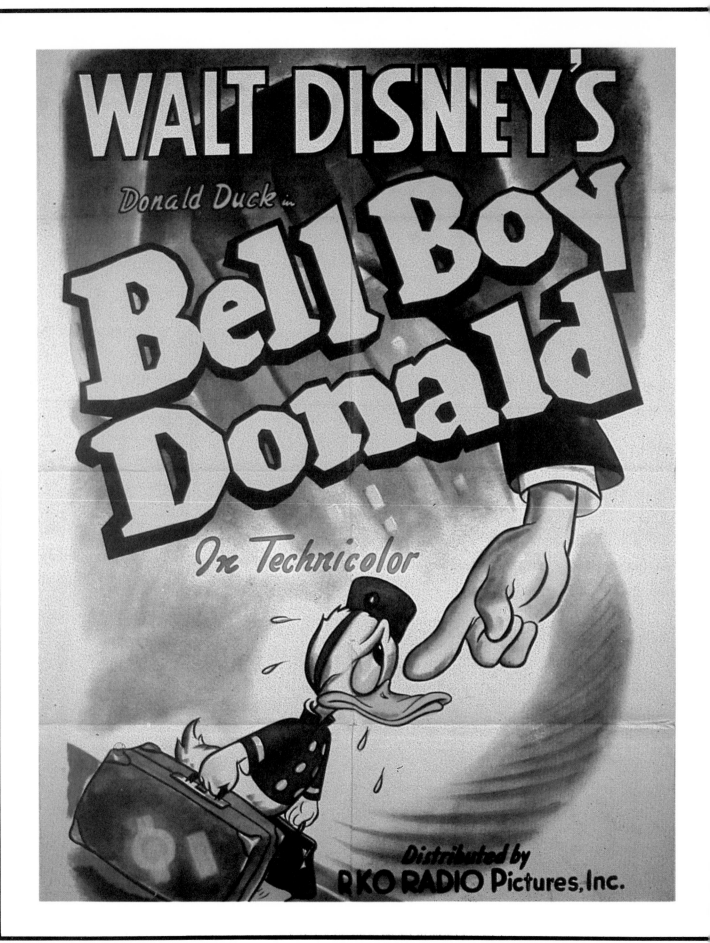

The Star

After his apprenticeship as Mickey's co-star, Donald made his own leap to stardom.

Below: Donald tries out a newfangled baby carriage in *Modern Inventions* (1937).

Hollywood films from time to time have been played by character actors of such importance that the hero and heroine were put after the title and the character actors in the starring position. Donald Duck may soon find himself in this unique position. . . .

If Mr. Disney is wise (probably the surest bet in motion pictures), he will keep his famous duck exactly as he is, and not overburden him with plot or circumstance. Donald Duck has at this moment one of the great historic appeals which only the films can produce. We hope he never becomes a comic cartoon on his own.

—from "The Rise of Donald Duck," 1936

L uckily for the world, this poor misguided writer never got his wish. In 1937 we find Donald already a star, having at last emerged from Mickey's shadow in a story called *Modern Inventions*. Although this film was released as a Mickey Mouse cartoon, the Mouse does not appear at all. Donald's supporting cast consists solely of nuts, bolts, and rivets.

Modern Inventions pits Donald against technology. He has come to a large exhibition hall where the newest mechanical wonders are on display and is unable to resist some easy

Another modern invention keeps its "eye" on baby Donald.

Overleaf: **A poster and selected scenes from *The Autograph Hound* (1939), a star-studded Hollywood spoof. On the right page Donald seems to break through the studio gates by riding with Greta Garbo. But closer examination from a different angle reveals his coolly clever ruse.**

mischief. Pushing buttons, pulling levers, turning cranks, he continues through the museum courting insult, injury, and disaster. Before the film ends he has had confrontations with a Cyclopean robot butler, a mechanical hitchhiker, an automatic bath-giver, been wrapped up in cellophane, attacked by a newfangled baby carriage, and given the "works" by a madly programmed barber chair.

It was a starring role with which Donald was most comfortable—that of the frustrated little man who can never get the best of a situation. But if he continued to play this kind of role, Donald was in serious danger of becoming typecast and therefore boring. With the help of his scriptwriters, he gradually began to broaden his scope and define a greater range of reactions. His rages became shorter and less frequent in subsequent cartoons, his smiles more and more engaging.

One explanation of Donald's evolution in the thirties was that he (along with the other Disney characters) was paralleling the growth and shifting values of America as it changed from predominantly rural to urban. After starting out as a barnyard character during the Depression, Donald was now leaving the farm to find his fortune in the cities; his co-starring roles show how he got into various forms of employment. In any case, the culture and ambitions of America during the late thirties offered

Donald a much wider choice of roles to reflect. He was quickly moving with the middle class into the life-style of the suburbs, but still had mass appeal as a worker (*Window Cleaners, Billposters, The Riveter*), an entrepreneur (*Donald's Dog Laundry*), sports enthusiast (*The Fox Hunt, Hockey Champ*), adventurer (*Polar Trappers, Sea Scouts*), public servant (*Officer Duck, Fire Chief, Truant Officer Donald*), and, in spite of his own Hollywood status, as a star-struck autograph seeker (*The Autograph Hound*).

Critics as well as audiences responded to this diversity in Donald's performances. A great deal of attention was paid to Donald's stardom in the press, most of it applauding his powerful acting and his ability to make audiences squirm in anticipation of a cathartic tantrum. The *New York Times*, hailing his artistic arrival, treated Donald with the same respect it accorded to all major figures—he was named in a headline as "Mister Donald Duck." Vicious attacks, such as the following one by *New Yorker* writer Russell Maloney, were atypical but indicative of the controversy and great passions that Donald could arouse. And in the long run, he probably benefited from the adverse publicity.

Another star who worries me is Donald Duck. Excellent as he is in supporting roles, I don't think Walt Disney was well-advised in elevating him to stardom. Donald Duck . . . represents the comedy of humor, a manifestation of formalism, if not decadence in the theatre. His is no more than personified irritability.

Decadence indeed! Nothing could have been further from the truth. During his early days as a star, Donald was devoted to his art, working hard to turn out his films on time, and constantly looking to improve himself. Several sources, including the *New York Times* of June 23, 1940, reported of Donald's great desire to be in one of Disney's full-length features. Much to his disappointment, Walt would not give him a role as one of the seven dwarfs in *Snow White*, but promised him a juicy part in the next feature production. Donald set about mastering every role in *Pinocchio*—including the lead, Geppetto, Jiminy Cricket, J. Worthington Foulfellow, Gideon, Monastro, Cleo, Figaro, the Coachman, the Blue Fairy—but failed to even make it to the first audition. Apparently, this was the only major conflict in an otherwise affectionate relationship between producer and star. Donald, in a real rage, threatened to tear up his contract and to picket every theater that showed *Pinocchio*.

lthough he *was* preoccupied with *Snow White*, Walt was not entirely neglecting his Duck. He realized that Donald, as Mickey did earlier, needed a supporting cast of players who could put him in new situations, point up unrevealed aspects of his personality, and add to the fun and excitement.

Opposite: **Admiral Donald takes the helm in *Sea Scouts* (1939).**

Above: **A year later, in *The Riveter* (1940), the star dangles precariously from a beam. This is a rare example of Donald done in airbrush.**

Good Scouts that they are, nephews Huey, Dewey, and Louie are always prepared for trouble with Unca Donald. Here they wrap up one of their funnier adventures, nominated for an Oscar in 1938.

Opposite: A 1954 publicity drawing shows Donald cutting his twentieth-birthday cake as the nephews look on in anticipation. Is the cake about to explode?

First to arrive on the scene were Donald's nephews, who accidentally thrust Donald into the role of "grown-up." Before this both children and adults had identified equally with an ageless Donald. Now there was the added dimension of taking sides. Children cheered each time Donald the authority figure was made to look ridiculous by Huey, Dewey, and Louie. Adults winced in recognition of their own little monsters.

As screen personalities, Huey, Dewey, and Louie were never fully realized. Their background was vague, they seemed to drift in and out of Donald's life, and when they did appear with Donald their behaviors were indistinguishable. Except for their different-colored clothing, the three nephews were identical in habits, looks, and speech to the point that in the early days they even shared their sentences. Huey would say the first few words, Dewey the next, and Louie the last—a cute cinematic device but a disastrous one. Jack Hannah put an end to the practice because it had a ruinous effect on a cartoon's timing. (Carl Barks reinstated split sentences in the comic books.)

What Huey, Dewey, and Louie did best was continue the family tradition as outrageous mischief-makers. Bright young imps who showed a remarkable aptitude for terrorist strategy, they were unrelenting in their harassment of Donald, whether he was working around the house or courting Daisy. Over the

years they inflicted on him innumerable injuries, including broken arms and legs and concussions, as well as severe loss of face. Their pranks against Donald did not appear to be motivated by a deep-seated hatred, but rather by the natural antagonism between parent and child or by the itching need to get even for a practical joke. The nephews' schemes, however simple or elaborate, were always carried out in a spirit of playfulness and fun—even the time they tried to convince Donald that he had died and become an angel (in *Soup's On,* they dress him up in flowing robes and halo while he is unconscious and hoist him up into the sky on a platform). And when the battle smoke cleared, the nephews could display thoughtfulness, affection, and loyalty that surprised even Donald. One cartoon depicted Donald punishing the nephews for having cigars—and then finding out they were his birthday present.

Donald treated Huey, Dewey, and Louie with a combination of malicious intent and love. His tricks against them were more impulsive than premeditated, and he often felt deep remorse and guilt at causing the nephews pain. Even after the worst rounds of mayhem, after being thoroughly outwitted and humiliated by the half-pint ducks, Donald was lenient when it came to punishment. Being a modern parent, he was much more likely to resort to psychology books.

In addition to their introductory story, the nephews figured prominently in *Hockey Champ, Truant Officer Donald, Lucky Number, Trick or Treat, Fountain of Youth,* and *Donald's Crime* (he steals money from their piggy bank for a date with Daisy!), but their best moments were still to come in another medium. In the hands of comic book artist Carl Barks, the nephews would acquire impressive new substance.

In 1939, another member of the family materialized. According to the Duck family tree from the Disney Archives, Gus Goose was a nephew of Luke the Goose, who had married Donald's Aunt Daphne (sister to his father Quackmore), and therefore was a very distant "cousin" to Donald. The genealogy is called into question by the note that Gus carries when he arrives at Donald's—it says that he is being sent to visit by an "Aunt Fanny." But whatever his origin, Gus is an unlikable character. Not only is he dumb (he is holding Donald's address upside down; rather than turning the piece of paper right side up to match the address on the mailbox, he turns the mailbox upside down), but he is exceedingly insensitive and greedy. To Donald's great annoyance, Gus interrupts while he is having dinner. The goose doesn't wait for an invitation—he thunders in like a Sherman tank, methodically destroying every morsel of food in Donald's house. Needless to say, Donald becomes irate and wages a valiant battle against his ill-mannered cousin. After this episode, Gus was no longer welcome in the Duck house. He never appeared again in a cartoon.

Opposite: **Cousin Gus in two stages.** *Above,* **as a line drawing on a character model sheet;** *below,* **as he finally appeared at Donald's doorstep.**

FINAL CLEANUP MODELS
ON GUS GOOSE
DONALD'S COUSIN GUS
RM-21

CHARACTER MODEL DEP'T.
O.K. by
NUMBER M64-A-
DATE 8-17-
© Walt Disney Prod.

-NOTE-
For further instructions
concerning these models,
see Wooley.

Carry
shadow turn
on Gus' body.

**W**hat Donald Duck needed most was a woman in his life. Once as Don Donald (1937), he had had a brief fling with Donna Duck—a coquettish señorita who, beneath her combs and mantilla and wildly fluttering eyelashes, bore a striking resemblance to her successor, Daisy. The affair was a tempestuous one, marked by ardent serenades, passionate kisses, explosive quarreling, and physical violence. Donna's temper proved to be an even match for Donald's, for in the course of a few minutes she slapped him, smashed a guitar over his head, threw him into a pool, and stomped a furious Mexican hat dance on his picture. Sometime later, when Donald arrived under her window at the wheel of a car, the fickle lady was in love again; this time it lasted until the car broke down. The independent (and well-prepared!) Donna pulled a unicycle out of her purse and pedaled out of Donald's life forever.

The encounter must have been traumatic for Donald. An entire three years passed before he was ready to face another woman. The momentous occasion was portrayed in *Mr. Duck Steps Out* (1940). It was the beginning of Donald's long-term relationship with none other than Daisy Duck.

When Donald first met her, Daisy was beautiful, vivacious, and an incredible flirt. Like Donna, she was adept at the art of eyelash-batting and could reduce Donald to mush with an adoring gaze or by whispering sweet nothings into his ear in a voice much like his own (Clarence Nash at work again, one octave up). On their first date, which was complicated by the pestering presence of Huey, Dewey, and Louie, Daisy and Donald found that they had much in common—especially that they were red-hot jitterbugs. The romance continued sporadically during the forties, but all indications are that Daisy had fallen hard for Donald. Donald's temporary rejection of her in *Donald's Dilemma* was so emotionally devastating that it sent her to see a psychiatrist. At this point, Daisy is extremely possessive of her man and unwilling to relinquish him to his newly found fame. When the psychiatrist asks her to decide to whom Donald should belong—her or the world—she screams without hesitation, "Me! Me! Me!" And once she had him where she wanted him, Daisy tried to make Donald over into her ideal man. *Cured Duck* tells how she became disgusted with Donald's temper and of his subsequent efforts to stay calm.

The problem with Daisy was that her character didn't develop much. Occasionally she had inspired moments, but her role as a traditional girlfriend confined her—her interactions with Donald were limited to domestic situations. One unusual episode was *Crazy Over Daisy* (1950), in which she wears Victorian garb (bustle and all) instead of her everyday blouse, heels, and perky pink bow. An even stranger transformation was her unducklike sultry voice (by this time different women from the Studio inking department were recording Daisy's voice). If an effort was being made to make Daisy more

Above: Donna Duck, the tempestuous señorita courted by Donald in *Don Donald* (1937).

Opposite: Daisy, the love of Donald's life, as she first appeared in *Mr. Duck Steps Out* (1940).

Overleaf: While Donald sits this one out, Daisy dances with all three nephews. They often proved an obstacle to Donald's and Daisy's romance, as was the case in *Mr. Duck Steps Out.*

In a scene from *Mr. Duck Steps Out*, Donald flirts with Daisy.

interesting, it did not succeed very well. This Daisy acted cold, aloof, even alien—impossible to connect with Donald.

Today, despite all odds, the romance still flourishes in the daily comic strips with no end—or marriage—in sight. Donald and Daisy's love has withstood forty years of anger, resentment, petty fights, practical jokes, broken dates, insults, and injuries, and we can only wonder why Daisy has never demanded a stronger commitment. Either she has the patience of a saint, the confidence that she doesn't need a husband, or a sneaking suspicion that a piece of paper will spoil all the fun. As for Donald, his attitude toward marriage was documented in *Donald's Diary*. After a dream about wedded "bliss" with Daisy, he wants no part of it.

With the addition of Daisy to the cast of supporting players, Donald's film ensemble was almost complete. When it was felt that the Duck could use some new antagonists, Jack Hannah dreamed up those rambunctious chipmunks, Chip and Dale. Audiences loved them—they were a minicomedy team in themselves as well as thorns in Donald's side. Some of their funniest adventures include *Winter Storage, Out on a Limb, Donald Applecore, Up a Tree*, and the 3-D cartoon, *Working for Peanuts*. At the same time Donald was getting bigger and bigger laughs from his bouts with smaller and smaller pests. After the chipmunks, he did battle with a musical bee (*Slide Donald Slide, Bee at the Beach, Bee on Guard, Let's Stick Together*) and some determined ants (*Tea for Two Hundred, Uncle Donald's Ants*). In episodes set in the forest, the challenges again grew bigger—Donald often met up with the Ranger or Humphrey the Bear.

The films of the late forties and fifties mark the last stage of Donald's character development. They present a more conservative Duck than we have seen before, settled into the responsibilities of being a parent and now taking part in a variety of suburban adventures: coping with the new neighbor, going to the beach, going hunting, hiking, combating ants, celebrating a birthday, matching wits with Chip and Dale, and occasionally courting Daisy. (Was it this humdrum life-style that drove him to so many exotic adventures in his comic books?) In his middle age Donald has developed the widest range of emotions yet to offset his basically angry nature. He experiences affection, jealousy, embarassment, regret, twinges of conscience, and shame, but he still gives in to his baser impulses to remain a mean practical joker, a sore sport, a poor loser, and given to powerful shows of temper, if not his former blind rages.

There were some offbeat cartoons in this era, among them *Donald's Dilemma* (the psychiatrist episode) and *Donald's Dream Voice*. In the latter, Donald is a traveling brush salesman who repeatedly is *given* the brush because he can't be understood. Women mock him and slam the door in his face—until he buys some "Ajax Voice Pills," which turn his garbled quacks into mellifluous, British-accented English. And then it's a different story. Housewives clamor for his brushes, and Donald, in a burst of confidence, decides to propose to Daisy. Just as he's about to take the last pill it rolls away from him, and a hilarious gag-filled chase ensues, ending with a contented cow mooing in a beautiful voice. A squawky proposal seems out of the question, and the cartoon closed with Donald hitting himself on the head.

This latter-day Donald is still frustrated...still unlucky... but a long way from the reprehensible character of *The Wise Little Hen*.

Ajax Voice Pills are Donald's salvation . . . for a while, in *Donald's Dream Voice* (1948).

Donald Duck and the Gorilla (1944).

Daddy Duck (1948).

Chef Donald (1941).

Donald's Double Trouble (1946).

Above and below: Frank Duck Brings 'Em Back Alive (1946).

Above and below: Donald's Dilemma **(1947).**

Clown of the Jungle (1947).

Tea for Two Hundred (1948).

Above and below: Soup's On (1948).

Slide, Donald, Slide (1949).

Toy Tinkers (1949).

Above and below: **Bee at the Beach** (1950).

Lucky Number (1951).

No Hunting (1955).

Donald in the War

Above and opposite: Scenes from *Donald Gets Drafted* (1942). Donald's war effort was greater than any other cartoon character's.

T he day after Pearl Harbor, the Army and Walt Disney joined forces as a result of a unilateral decision on the part of the U.S. high command. A seven-hundred-man antiaircraft unit assigned to protect nearby defense plants ensconced itself on the Disney lot and turned the only sound stage into a repair shop. Disney was contacted by the Navy with a request to produce some educational films about aircraft spotting. These films marked the Studio's entry into the war effort and the beginning of a new era in which Disney moved more and more toward live action.

As one of Hollywood's biggest box-office attractions, Donald Duck knew that he had to do his part for America. After all, Gable and Jimmy Stewart and David Niven were in uniform and Betty Grable and Rita Hayworth were doing their best to help the fighting boys keep their spirits up. So Donald, too, went above and beyond the call of duty—the spunky little duck was there throughout every battle and every dark moment of the war, serving as a symbol of American determination. And at last his inordinate belligerence found a nationally acceptable target.

Ironically, Donald never got to enlist. As it happened, he was drafted even before the United States entered the war, as

March 24, 1941
(Date of mailing)

┌─────────────────────────┐
│   │
│   (STAMP OF LOCAL BOARD) │
└─────────────────────────┘

ORDER TO REPORT FOR INDUCTION

The President of the United States,

To ___ Donald ___ Fauntleroy ___ Duck ___
(First name)   (Middle name)   (Last name)

Order No. ___ 13 ___

GREETING:

Having submitted yourself to a Local Board composed of your neighbors for the purpose of determining your availability for training and service in the armed forces of the United States, you are hereby notified that you have now been selected for training and service in the ___ Army ___
(Army, Navy, Marine Corps)

You will, therefore, report to the Local Board named above at ___ Soldiers Walk & Generals Drive ___,
(Place of reporting)

at ___ 4:02 ___ A. m., on the ___ 1st ___ day of ___ April ___, 19 41

DONALD GETS DRAFTED

shown by an induction (or was that inducktion?) notice dated March 24, 1941. In *Donald Gets Drafted*, released in 1942, he went through the comic but harrowing experiences with which millions of men could sympathize. There on the screen was Donald Duck submitting to an assembly line physical, getting measured for an ill-fitting uniform, quivering before a monster of a drill instructor, and marching until his feet were ready to fall off. He, of course, had envisioned a tour of duty in which he would be constantly surrounded by amorous WACs powerless to resist a dashing Duck in uniform. Still, patriot that he was, Donald wouldn't let basic training get him down. He bravely went on to the greater glories of military adventure in *The Vanishing Private, Sky Trooper, Fall Out, Fall In, The Old Army Game,* and *Commando Duck*.

When a new law went into effect in 1942, fifteen million Americans became eligible to pay income taxes for the first time. The Treasury Department commissioned Disney to produce an upbeat film that would explain the government's use of the money and encourage voluntary and speedy payment with a minimum of resentment. Donald

Above and below: Donald submits to a grueling physical and then, for all his modesty, measures up to G.I. standards in *Donald Gets Drafted* (1942).

Poster for *The Vanishing Private* (1942).

Duck was awarded the starring role in *The New Spirit*, but only after Disney himself came to his defense. As told by Richard Schickel in *The Disney Version*, the making of *The New Spirit* involved quite a battle behind the scenes:

Disney rushed to Washington for conferences, rushed home to begin planning the film, which starred Donald Duck, then rushed back east with the storyboards...to show the Secretary of the Treasury, Henry J. Morgenthau, Jr.... [Morgenthau] was unimpressed. He had hoped Disney would create a new character, a sort of Mr. Average Taxpayer, who would take a somewhat more sober tack than the duck did in dramatizing the virtues of paying taxes in full and on time. Disney argued for making the painful business seem to be as much fun as possible. The Secretary countered by claiming that he did not like Donald Duck. There are at least two versions of Disney's reply, but in effect he noted with some heat that his giving the Treasury the duck was the equivalent of MGM's giving the Treasury Clark Gable; he was the studio's top star. Morgenthau finally yielded...."

The New Spirit opens with Donald listening to a radio that bellows, "Our shores have been attacked!" and instructs him to do his part by paying the $13.00 tax he owes on his income of $2,900.14. Eager to help, he fills out the form and personally rushes his money to Washington. There, as his piles of coins dissolve into smokestacks, Donald literally sees his taxes go to work in an awesome sequence regarded as a potent piece of propaganda.

A powerful blend of terrifying images and soul-stirring words, the second half of *The New Spirit* depicts proud and defiant firebreathing defense factories working overtime to combat monstrous enemy planes, battleships, and submarines. As aircraft and ships are destroyed by American might, the radio blares forth an ominous warning with an unforgettable refrain: "Taxes to sink the Axis!"..."Taxes to bury the Axis!"..."Taxes to beat to earth the evil destroyer of freedom and peace!" When the smoke of the last exploded enemy submarine clears and the strains of Beethoven's victory theme from the Fifth Symphony fade from the background, the sky settles into a glorious pattern of stars and stripes. "Taxes will keep American democracy on the march" assures the radio voice, with a heavenly chorus of *America* swelling behind it.

Apparently the message was more than well received. The *New York Times* praised the film as "a novel attraction...a thoroughly agreeable inducement to a tough task." More important, though, was the response of the public, for that year taxes were reported to have come in more promptly than ever. The only ones unhappy with *The New Spirit* were the members of Congress who refused to appropriate $80,000 for the film, which left the Treasury to get the cash elsewhere and Disney in the red. The next year *The New Spirit* was revised as *The Spirit*

Opposite: In *The Spirit of '43*, one voice of Donald's conscience exhorts him to save money for taxes, while the other encourages him to splurge!

Overleaf: Those who missed *The New Spirit* in the theaters were treated to the opening sequence in an issue of *Look* magazine.

The NEW SPIRIT

© WALT DISNEY

1. "YES - THERE IS A NEW SPIRIT IN AMERICA TODAY"

2. RADIO - "THE SPIRIT OF A FREE PEOPLE UNITED AGAIN IN A COMMON CAUSE"

THAT'S RIGHT!
3. RADIO - "TO STAMP TYRANNY FROM THE EARTH"

4. "OUR VERY SHORES HAVE BEEN ATTACKED"

5. "THAT'S NOT RIGHT !!!"

6. "YOUR WHOLE COUNTRY IS MOBILIZING FOR TOTAL WAR"

SWISH
7. RADIO - "YOUR COUNTRY NEEDS YOU !"

8.

9. "O.K. — I'M READY !"

10. "ARE YOU A PATRIOTIC AMERICAN ?"

YES! SIR!
11. RADIO - "EAGER TO DO YOUR PART - ?"

12. RADIO - "TO PRESERVE OUR FREEDOM ?"

WHO? ME?
13. RADIO - "THEN THERE IS SOMETHING IMPORTANT YOU CAN DO — "

14. "OH BOY - OH BOY - I'LL DO IT !!!"

15. "YOU WON'T GET A MEDAL FOR DOING IT"

16. "OH - THAT'S ALL RIGHT"

17. RADIO - "IT MAY MEAN A SACRIFICE ON YOUR PART."

18. "I'LL DO IT ANYWAY !"

19. RADIO - "BUT IT WILL BE A VITAL HELP TO YOUR COUNTRY IN THIS HOUR OF NEED"

of '43 with a brand-new beginning, showing Donald torn between spending his money on a night on the town and saving it for taxes.

In addition to volunteering his services and encouraging Americans to pay their taxes and buy war bonds, Donald Duck made one of his biggest contributions to the war effort by appearing on over 400 insignia that the Disney Studio designed, free of charge, for the military. Donald, more than any other of his fellow cartoon characters, symbolized the gutsy, fists-up fighting spirit of the American soldier and so became the mascot and good luck charm of innumerable units and squadrons. On planes, tanks, jeeps, and uniforms, Donald was found riding torpedoes and bombs, destroying submarines, carrying mines, giving his all to stop the enemy. He was usually portrayed with his characteristic glare (which alone was powerful enough to sink a battleship) or a smug grin of triumph. Military command hailed him as a tremendous morale builder.

Donald's greatest wartime achievement, however, was *Der Fuehrer's Face*, released on January 1, 1943. Originally conceived as an aid to sell war bonds, this satiric anti-Nazi cartoon was an overwhelming success and went on to win the Academy Award as Best Cartoon Short Subject of 1942–43. It also became famous for the irreverent theme song that the nation gleefully added to its arsenal of fighting music. "Der Fuehrer's Face," with its sassy lyrics and its chorus punctuated by Bronx cheers, became an instant hit in the forties, aided by a wacky Spike Jones recording, and since then has become an evocative reminder of the war era. Novelists and screenwriters striving for authenticity often work the song into their scenes of that period.

The plot of *Der Fuehrer's Face* focuses on Donald's miserable existence as a Nazi. He is seen being forced to salute pictures of Hitler, Mussolini, and Hirohito ("Aw, *heil!*" he mutters dejectedly—a sly pun on "Aw, hell!"), goose-stepping among a corps of porcine Germans, reluctantly building his body to strengthen the master race, working feverishly on an assembly line, and living in a thoroughly Nazi-fied land where the topiary is swastika-shaped and even the facade of a slant-roofed house bears an eerie resemblance to Hitler. The reason for the nightmarish landscape is just that—Donald has only been having a horrible dream and wakes up, in star-spangled pajamas, joyously proclaiming his love for the U.S.A.

In 1943 Donald was working on yet another front. That was the year he became a goodwill ambassador to South America, starring in the feature film *Saludos Amigos* (*Hello Friends,* or as renowned critic Bosley Crowther translated it in Donald's style of speech, *Hiya Pals*). With the war raging in Europe, America—and especially Holly-

Disney Studios designed over 400 insignia for the U.S. Government during the war. Requests for the emblems grew so numerous that the Studio once had five men drawing them.

Above: Joe Carioca and Panchito pose for a publicity shot with Donald and Walt.

wood—was looking for new economic markets to offset its losses. As part of its newly established Good Neighbor Policy, the State Department had sponsored a trip by Disney and some of his staff to Venezuela, Chile, Argentina, and Brazil in 1941. Disney intended to produce some cartoons inspired by these colorful countries, but the idea of separate cartoons was abandoned, on the reasoning that each could only be released in the country with which it dealt. The enforced solution to the problem was to link the four shorts together with 16 mm color "home movies" that had been taken of Disney and his entourage during the trip. A live-action travelogue/animated musical fantasy resulted that was warmly received both here and in South America. *Saludos Amigos* opened there in 1942 and in the United States in February 1943.

Donald's first appearance in *Saludos* is as a typical American tourist in Bolivia. To the accompaniment of lilting native flute music, he explores the native sights, visits Lake Titicaca, and rents a llama ("one of the haughtiest characters the Disney boys have ever drawn," remarked Crowther) to travel through the mountains. Just when it seems that all is

Opposite: The sheet music for *Der Fuehrer's Face.*

Above and opposite: **Two movie posters for *Saludos Amigos* (1943).**

going well, Donald and the llama reach a narrow rope bridge spanning a valley that appears to be miles below. As the two begin a frantic competition to get across, planks give way and for a moment Donalds clings to his life by a thread. Ranting and raving, he stops to listen to a voice-over calmly reminding him that "one should never lose one's temper." "Ahh, shaddup!" is Donald's not-so-measured reply. Iris out.

In the following segments, the Disney troupe continues its live-action travels interspersed with two more cartoons, "Pedro" and "El Gaucho Goofy," respectively featuring a whimsical little mailplane named Pedro and the ever-hapless Goofy attempting to become a hero of the Pampas. Finally, Donald returns to star in what is easily the best part of the forty-three-minute film. "Aquarela do Brasil" ("Watercolor of Brazil") unfolds a dazzling finale glowing with vibrant color, pulsing with Latin rhythms, abounding in crazy animation gags, and, best of all, introducing that debonair Brazilian jitterbird, Joe (sometimes known as José) Carioca.

It's Carnival time in Rio. The cartoon opens with an exquisite sequence of animated watercoloring. Stepping into the action, one of the artists sketches a suave, Havana-cigar-smoking parrot clothed in a dapper white jacket and a jaunty

Caramba! Joe Carioca salutes his amigo Donald.

Panama hat. Fast-talking, wisecracking Joe Carioca comes to life and whisks a wide-eyed Donald off on a tour of South America. A self-propelled animated paintbrush fills in the backgrounds as they go along; at one point Donald stumbles into it and gets covered with blue paint. This funny, fast-paced sequence climaxes with Joe Carioca teaching Donald the samba to the tunes "Brazil" and "Tico, Tico." The two feathered friends dance off for a spirited night on the town, cooling their Carnival fever with the attentions of some pretty señoritas.

The critical reaction to *Saludos Amigos* was as favorable as the public's. Crowther praised its total effect as "one of ascending enthusiasm," and went on to say:

As always in Mr. Disney's pictures, the quality of the humor is bright and sly, with touches of gentle satire laced in with jovial fun...the title song is a dandy, and the samba, "Aquarela do Brasil" is an air which would limber the muscles and warm the blood of a petrified fish....It isn't what you would call a factual film, but it certainly does well by South America...And Joe Carioca—well, we just must see more of him.

Critics Howard Barnes called it "a brilliant job of picture making" and John T. McManus acknowledged that it did "a job in hemisphere relations that no one before had managed to achieve." By becoming a tourist, Donald Duck had shown South America how good a neighbor Uncle Sam was and given North America a fascinating introduction to a little-known continent. The travelogue/cartoon format transformed lessons in foreign geography, culture, and customs into sheer entertainment.

But *Saludos Amigos* was only the first overture toward capturing the goodwill of South America. Disney had another, more ambitious South American extravaganza in the works, expanding on the last part of *Saludos*. In 1945, *The Three Caballeros* was released. Although the film had been completed earlier than *Saludos*, the priorities of war had made it impossible for Disney to get color prints any sooner.

The Three Caballeros marked the first combination of live action and animation since Walt and Ub Iwerks (who worked on the process effects in *Caballeros*) had done the *Alice in Cartoonland* series in the twenties. But now it was billed as "the most startling advance in motion picture technique since the advent of sound." This technique made the film seem less disjointed than *Saludos Amigos,* but still allowed the live-action appearances of the leading South American stars, Aurora Miranda of Brazil and Dora Luz and Carmen Molina of Mexico. Incorporating a variety of artistic styles—from lush, slow-moving tableaux to frenetically paced animation liberally laced with incredible visual puns to mind-boggling surrealism—*The Three Caballeros* evoked almost as much controversy as

Walt and two of his artists confer on *Saludos Amigos*. Behind them is the storyboard for the cartoon.

Fantasia. Today this outstanding work of imagination and artistic technique has earned a new reputation among film buffs. Film expert Leonard Maltin attributes the attention to the fact that it was "years ahead of its time in conception and execution, and more in tune with the free-form animation of today than that of the 1940s."

Like *Saludos Amigos, The Three Caballeros* weaves together several separate cartoons. This time the unifying element is the quintessential Disney adventurer Donald Duck, who has just received a giant gift-wrapped package for his birthday. As he opens each box, the gifts transform themselves into wonderfully entertaining stories. Adding to the excitement, every frame is beautiful South American scenery, a steady beat of hip-shaking music, and explosions of tropical color that can only leave one gasping.

Overleaf: **On the left is the Spanish language poster for *Three Caballeros* (1945), on the right, the American version.**

139

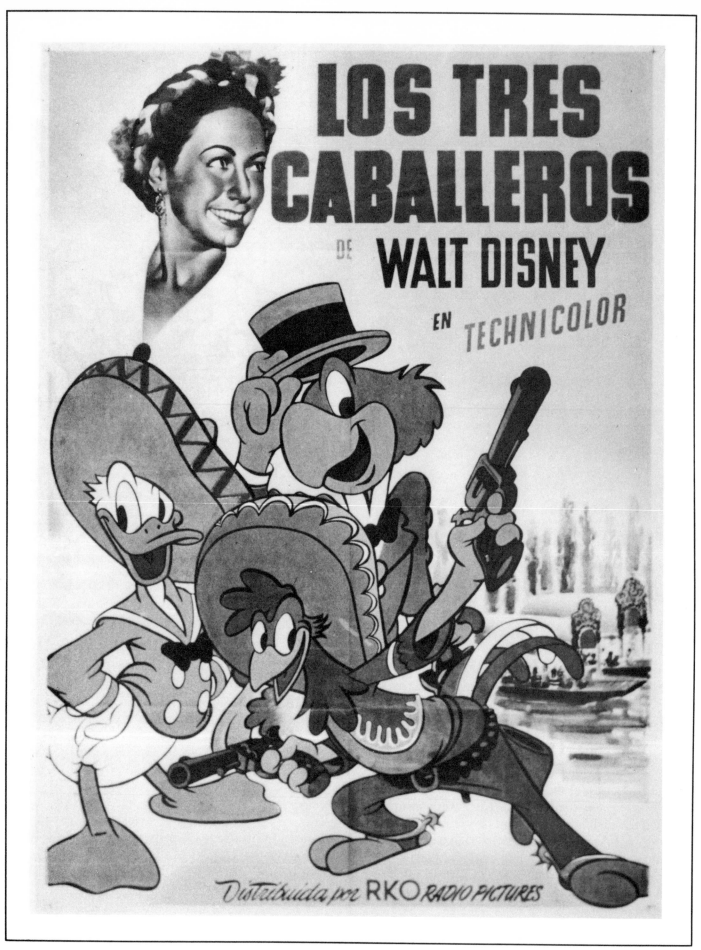

The crazy Aracuan bird first appeared in "Aves Raras" in *Three Caballeros*. He reappeared in *Blame It on the Samba* in 1948.

Donald's first gift is a movie projector. He snaps on a reel and settles back to watch "Aves Raras," a diverting little lesson on South American birds. Along with Pablo, the sad little penguin who hates the cold, we meet the marvelously loco Aracuan bird whose rapid-fire antics include walking off the movie screen to shake hands with Donald. Next on the bill is the tale of Little Gauchito, who finds a flying burrito and enters the fantastical creature in a local race. Then Donald opens another present, a book on Brazil, and the relentlessly raucous fun and frolicking begins.

"Joe Carioca!" yells Donald in happy amazement. The "bad boy" of the tropics has stepped out of the pop-up book in Donald's hands. Joe is so happy to see his old friend that at one point he is literally beside himself—he splits into four birds! With the help of a sledgehammer, Joe brings Donald down to his own diminutive book size. The two hop back into the pop-up book, in which a train appears to take them to Baía, Brazil. To the strains of a hauntingly beautiful song, Donald finds romance there in the arms of Latin lovely Aurora Miranda. They dance, they sway, they flirt—the Duck is hopelessly smitten! When at last the señorita kisses him, Donald blows a fuse, with the screen reflecting his sensory overload in a psychedelic display of color, music, and live-action dancing. Even the background houses and streets move to the music. But at last Donald and Joe come to their senses, jump out of the book, and return to full size.

Next it's on to gay old Mexico, where an unusual visualization of the sound track becomes so wild and explosive that a new character, Panchito the rootin'-tootin' charro rooster, bursts forth brandishing his guns. The fowl play reaches its height here as the three sing their peppy theme song, "The Three Caballeros." After a short discourse on Mexican traditions, Panchito produces a piñata for Donald to smash. Out falls a storybook that interpolates further Mexican culture and history; flying on a magic serape, the three birds visit the scenes in the book.

The end of *Caballeros* resounds with the sights and sounds of fiestas and a trip to Acapulco in which Donald—now an outrageous ladies' man—cavorts with an entire beach full of bathing beauties. One of them, Dora Luz, serenades Donald with "You Belong to My Heart." The Duck takes flight into another spectacular fantasy, dancing among the stars, watching everything before his eyes metamorphose into neon signs, then flowers, geometric shapes, and, finally, silhouettes. The breathtaking action continues with a Busby Berkeley-like chorus-girl sequence, stops only for a moment, and resumes with Carmen Molina's appearance to dance the famous "Jesusita" joined by Donald and a group of cacti. Too charged up to stop playing around, Donald and his amigos engage in a mock bullfight, which leads to a megaton blast of a fireworks ending.

"Dazzles and numbs the senses without making any sense"

said Crowther in his initial review. "Flashy and exciting—and no more." Only a few days later, his hostility toward the film had intensified. Writing in the Sunday *Times*, he spoke of "cartoon technique to perfection without any consistent artistry. As a matter of fact, it is a *chef d'oeuvre* of artistic anarchy...."

Other critics agreed, but in spite of the adverse criticism, *The Three Caballeros* thoroughly delighted North and South American audiences and must be seen as one of Donald Duck's finest hours. It was yet another example of how the Duck could rise above his selfish urges and impatient nature, how he could put aside his own concerns for the good of his country.

Let it be remembered that in the 1940s, Donald Duck was a bona fide American Hero.

Below: **Weary and webfoot-sore, Donald trudges toward victory.**

Scenes from the Oscar-winning cartoon *Der Fuehrer's Face* show Donald's nightmare existence in "Nutzi Land."

In *The Spirit of '43* Donald decides to abandon selfishness and pull for victory.

Commando Duck (1944) in action!

Donald surveys the Bolivian scene in *Saludos Amigos* (1943).

Take it away, José! Donald and Joe Carioca sway to a Latin rhythm.

The *Three Caballeros* in their snappy sombreros.

Donald flexes his bulging biceps for the admiring senoritas.

Above and below: During the war years Donald became an outrageous flirt, as shown in *Three Caballeros*.

Gallery of Old Masters

What was there to work on after the last drawing of a cartoon was done? What did an in-betweener do in between?

To amuse themselves when there was some free time, Disney animators envisioned Donald Duck as if he had been painted by old and modern masters. Freed from the necessity to work only in gray pencil, they reveled in the colors used by Rembrandt, Degas, Gauguin, and others. "We stuck to one medium," said one animator, "color pencils, and tried to simulate pastels, tempera, oil and watercolors with the pencils at hand."

This classic series began in 1941 with *Madonna Duck* (it was employed as a gag in *The Reluctant Dragon*). By 1945, sixteen more masterpieces had been completed, forming an invaluable contribution to art history. *Life* magazine noted the achievement by featuring the paintings in its April 16 issue.

And when the animators tired of imitating the Old Masters, they began to suggest dramatic roles for Donald. One can only imagine the box office records that would have been set had *Gone With the Duck* been produced.

Madonna Duck (da Vinci)

Portrait of a Venetian Quack (Tintoretto)

Lady Daisy Duck (Rubens)

Venus and a "Donald Duck" (Titian)

Soup's On (Brueghel)

Duck with a Glove (Frans Hals)

Don with A Pink (Quentin Massys)

Pinkie Daisy (Sir Thomas Lawrence)

El Quacko (El Greco)

Two Duck Dancers (Degas)

The Blue Duck (Gainsborough)

Tahitian Ducks (Gauguin)

Don's Whistling Mother (Whistler)

Modern Quack (Picasso)

Harem Duck (Matisse)

Vincent Van Duck, Self-Portrait (Van Gogh)

The Noble Snob (Rembrandt)

Gone With the Duck

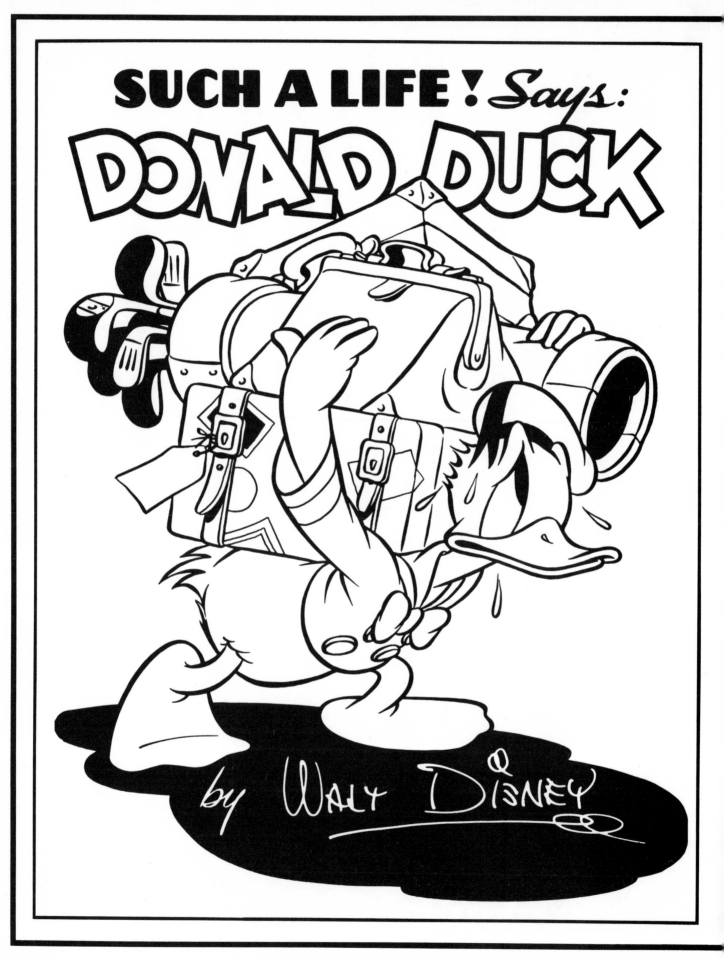

Books and Strips

Donald became a best-seller with a wide variety of books, including the Big Little Books, which measured 3¾" x 4½".

Opposite and overleaf: An excerpt from the first Donald Duck book (1935).

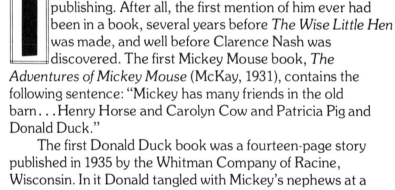

I t was fitting that Donald Duck became a star of book publishing. After all, the first mention of him ever had been in a book, several years before *The Wise Little Hen* was made, and well before Clarence Nash was discovered. The first Mickey Mouse book, *The Adventures of Mickey Mouse* (McKay, 1931), contains the following sentence: "Mickey has many friends in the old barn...Henry Horse and Carolyn Cow and Patricia Pig and Donald Duck."

The first Donald Duck book was a fourteen-page story published in 1935 by the Whitman Company of Racine, Wisconsin. In it Donald tangled with Mickey's nephews at a swimming hole. Publishers who had initially rejected the idea of Disney characters as book subjects discovered that Donald had the magic ingredients that made a bestseller. Soon a number of houses (Dell, Whitman, Simon & Schuster, Random House, Grosset & Dunlap) began marketing the Duck in every conceivable way—storybooks, picture books, shape books (die-cut around the cover art rather than in the conventional rectangle), pop-up books, paint books; Top-Top Tales, Big Tell-a-Tales, Little Golden Books, Big Golden Books, Cozy Corner Books, and so forth. Especially popular were Whitman's Big Little Books and Better Little Books—child-sized illustrated volumes that measured 3¾ inches by 4½ inches and contained as many as 424 pages. Stories ran the gamut from *Donald Duck and His Friends* to *Donald Duck and Ghost Morgan's Treasure* to *Donald Duck and the Mystery of the Double X.*

As it was a very warm summer day, Donald Duck sat on the front porch of his houseboat, fanning himself. As he rocked back and forth in his chair he hummed a little duck melody.

Meanwhile Mickey Mouse's two little nephews scampered along the path to Donald Duck's house. They played tag and other games and were very gay dancing along the water's edge.

Soon they came to Donald Duck's house-boat and when they saw Donald sitting on the porch, they called to him, "We want to go swimming! Please, Uncle Donald, take us swimming!"

"Not a chance," replied Donald. "I'd rather swim with two crocodiles than with you two." "I thought almost everyone could swim," said one of Mickey's nephews. "Donald Duck must be a sissy."

"Who's a sissy? Who says I can't swim?" quacked Donald, loudly. "All my family are champion swimmers, and I'm the champion of my family! Just you wait until I get my swimming suit!"

Mickey's nephews clapped their hands in glee. They told Donald that they would meet him at the swimming pool, and off they skipped down the path, laughing and shouting.

Arriving at the swimming pool, they put on their bathing suits and began their mischief. They moved the diving board from deep water to shallow water, where the pool was not over six inches deep.

Then the nephews lay on their backs, the shallow water hiding everything but their heads and their toes. They looked as if floating in deep water. "Show us how to dive, Donald!" they cried.

"Is the water deep?" Donald asked. "It's over your head!" the two nephews answered. "Okay, then," Donald exclaimed. "Here's a dive such as you've never seen before! Ready? One - TWO - THREE!"

With a big spring, Donald bounced high into the air. Then down he came, head first, his nose pointing right for the water and the splash. But instead of a splash there was a SCRUNCH!

There was Donald—his head stuck into the soft mud, and his tail feathers wiggling high in the air. Mickey's nephews laughed long and loud: "See, Uncle Donald, we told you the water was over your head!"

When Donald finally freed his head, he stood up. He was very angry. "What's the matter, Uncle Donald?" Mickey's nephews asked innocently. "Oh, boy!" quacked Donald. "That water's HARD!"

The comic strip career of Donald Duck began at the same time as his entry into book publishing. After the film release of *The Wise Little Hen,* the story ran in Sunday papers as part of the *Silly Symphony* comic strip series. Donald made his initial appearance on September 16, 1935, and the story ran for about three months. Soon after, Donald's popularity was rewarded with a strip written by Ted Osborne and penciled and inked by the master of the Donald Duck comic strip, Al Taliaferro. The Silly Symphony Sunday color page "Featuring Donald Duck" was begun on August 30, 1936. Sometime before the end of the series the first part of the title was dropped and only "Donald Duck" remained in the title panel.

An interesting and little-known fact about this 1937 strip is that three familiar ducklings made their debut there under the same circumstances as they would later appear in the cartoon *Donald's Nephews.* In this version we get a solid reason for their presence at the Duck house, but even more important, *we get evidence that the kids have a father!* "Dear Donald," writes cousin Della (she was "Dumbella" in the film), "I am sending your angel nephews Louie, Huey, and Dewey to stay with you while their father is in the hospital. A giant firecracker exploded under his chair . . . the little darlings are so playful. . . ." Several

The Wise Little Hen reappeared in 1935 as a comic strip in the Silly Symphony series that ran in the Sunday papers.

weeks later, the nephews return to Della, having blithely provoked Donald to the point of near madness.

Donald continued to appear on the Silly Symphony page until December 5, 1937. The page itself continued until as late as 1951, often as a showcase for Disney movie characters who weren't prime comic strip material. Bambi, Snow White and the Seven Dwarfs, Cinderella, to name a few, all had very short runs. Joe Carioca lasted two years, and the other caballero, Panchito, entertained in a year-long series.

Donald was such a hit in the Silly Symphony Sunday series that on February 7, 1938, he was made star of his own daily strip syndicated by King Features. In his first week he started out as a hostile zookeeper, returned to the scene of *Alpine Climbers,* and then settled down to the problems of his suburban world, where flat tires, crookedly hung pictures, and long lines at commuter bus stops were the frustrations to be reckoned with. From the very first strip until July 12, 1974, Bob Karp dreamed up Donald's predicaments; Al Taliaferro made them come alive until he passed away in 1969. They also teamed up for the Sunday color comics which began on December 10, 1939.

Recurring themes included the familiar—Donald painting himself into some kind of corner, stranded on a desert island, going fishing, dealing with household disasters or neighborhood shopkeepers. The Duck, with his impatient nature and constant bad luck was well suited for these problematic situations. Mickey, for instance, could never have carried them off so believably.

Donald was not always alone in his comic strip realm. New and old family, neighbors, and a full complement of anonymous, dog-faced extras populated his world, alternately giving him ideas, trouble, and someone to talk to. As could be expected with this format, certain characters worked better than others. Gus the Goose was no more successful and no less hungry than he was in films; the nephews were amusing though not as malicious and spunky; the neighboring Joneses came into play only for the convenience of gags. Most outstanding in the daily strips was Daisy, who finally established herself as a woman of character.

When Donald first met Daisy in the strips she had just moved into his neighborhood. She was still the flirt she had been in films, and their dates were spent in romantic hours sitting on the couch. It only took a short while, however, before Daisy became what might later be described as a typical TV sit-com girlfriend/wife of the '50s—a scatterbrain scheming for Donald's attention, fighting with him over petty things, flying into jealous rages and expressing her anger through physical and verbal abuse. Nor could she rise above stereotyped notions about the behavior of women. Among other offenses, Daisy was a notoriously bad driver, disaster on the golf course, and afflicted with a weakness for silly hats which at times drove Donald to distraction. Early in the seventies Daisy joined a women's

Donald's name was first added to the Silly Symphony title panel in 1936. It later became the most prominent part of the panel.

GRANDMA DUCK

GRANDMA'S BILL IS SHORTER THAN DONALD'S

AVOID SPRADDLE-LEGGED POSES—

EYE AREA NOT AS WIDE AS DONALD'S

The only woman other than Daisy to appear as a regular in Donald's comic strips was Grandma Duck.

group, which failed to raise her consciousness. In a 1976 strip she was still preparing dinner, while Donald—male chauvinist duck that he is—sat in an easy chair and waited.

Some years later, another woman entered Donald's life. She was Grandma Duck, a genuine old-fashioned lady who delighted in living in the past. Clad in high-buttoned shoes and high-collared, leg-o-mutton-sleeved jackets, Grandma Duck struck terror into the hearts of her relatives by voicing such commands as: "So, idling again! Go sweep the walks! Evil finds work for idle hands." She was a strict authoritarian who disapproved of sloth, dirt, immoral behavior, Daisy's decolletage and miniskirts, and milk that came out of bottles. After a while, Grandma's unsettling visits became more and more infrequent. She has not appeared in the strips for several years.

In 1961 Professor Ludwig von Drake of television fame joined the family, usually to astound Donald with his latest invention. Von Drake was often working on the perfect alarm clock (one silent model squirted cold water as a wake-up call, another emitted the scents of bacon and coffee), a contraption for the golf course, or walking about aimlessly with his mind full

From Coast to Coast...
243 Daily **DONALD DUCK** Comic Strips
109 Sunday **DONALD DUCK** Color Pages
in newspapers across the country
Total Circulation- 28,000,000

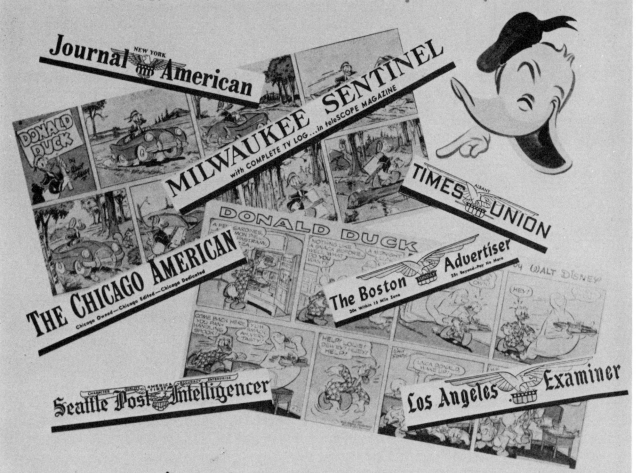

BUT THAT'S NOT ALL...
In 1960 we're tying DONALD DUCK to DISNEYLAND...
the most fabulous place in the world

A sales promotion piece for Donald's comic strips.

The absentminded professor Ludwig von Drake was invented for television but was a popular comic-strip figure from 1961 on.

Opposite: **The first week of Donald Duck daily strips appeared in February of 1938.**

of mathematical equations. Even when his inventions backfired on Donald (as they invariably did), he was a harmless and amusing character to have around the house—although considerably less colorful without his Austrian accent.

The last character to join the comic strip family was Uncle Scrooge McDuck. He had been around since 1947, but did not debut in the strips until 1964. Donald was working for the old miser then and many of the strips show his attempts to get a raise. While this Scrooge is portrayed as money-mad and stingy, the presence and awesomeness of his wealth is not as acutely felt in the strips as in the comic books. Without the money bin, the daily swims, the paeans to pennies or the threats to his lucky dime, we never get the feeling of how intimate McDuck is with his uncountabillions; in the comic strips we never see him as anything more than "the big boss." At least once both Uncle Scrooge and Professor von Drake took part in the same strip on a fishing expedition. The meeting was not a particularly memorable one. These characters work better with Donald than with one another.

Overall, just as in the films, there was a noticeable evolution of Donald in the comic strips. It wasn't merely that he was drawn by different artists, but the humor itself changed over the years. In the beginning the gags were largely visual, re-enacting the plights Donald was experiencing in his cartoons. Even when there was expository dialogue in the opening, the last panel was most often silent. We saw Donald looking askance at Huey, Dewey, and Louie, "drinking" soup from an atomizer, standing on his head to get a better perspective on modern art, or putting a firecracker into a suggestion box at work.

In later years, with the change of writers, wisecracking became a staple of the comics. "Why haven't you ever considered marriage, Uncle Scrooge?" asks Daisy in a 1975 strip. "I have. . . ." replies the uncle. "I *consider* it a nuisance." "But a bachelor has nobody to share his troubles with," Daisy persists. "Why should a bachelor *have* any troubles?" is Scrooge's final quip on the subject.

Other examples of this type of humor include von Drake's diet shampoo for fatheads and Donald's eagle on the golf course—a bird who had to be taken to the hospital. Or consider this smart-aleck exchange between Donald and Scrooge: "I deserve a larger paycheck." "I agree. Is eleven by fourteen enough?"

Today, the daily gags continue to be enjoyed by millions both here and abroad. It must be noted that they were crucial to Donald Duck's development as a celebrity because the earliest Karp/Taliaferro efforts went into the first Walt Disney comic books. Once Donald made the leap into the world of Superman and Wonder Woman, he too became a Superhero. With another identity and fantastic adventures, it was as if a star had been reborn.

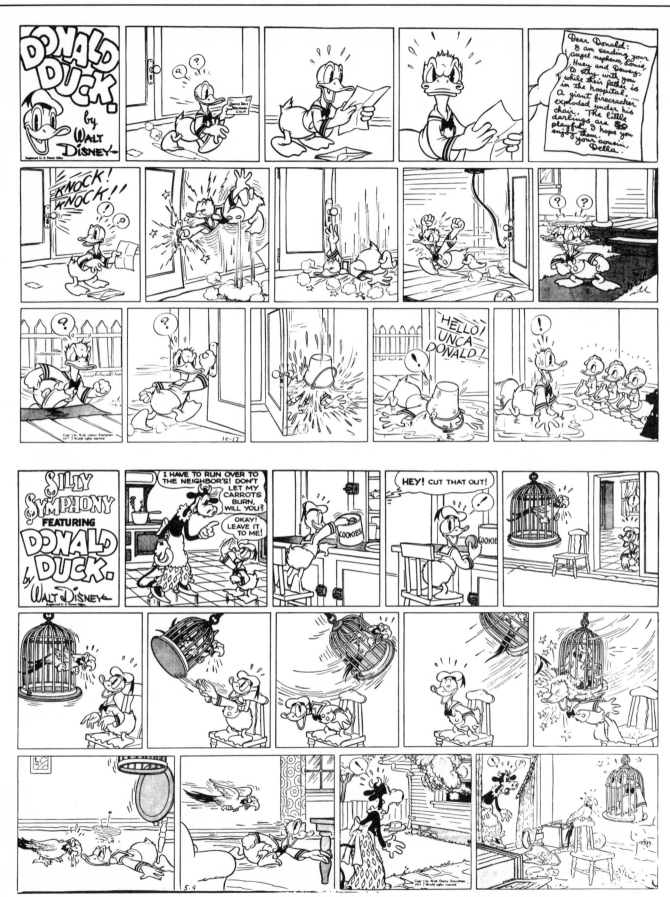

Above: Two early Sunday strips from 1937. Written by Ted Osborne; penciled and inked by Al Taliaferro.

DONALD DUCK ⋅:⋅ ⋅:⋅ ⋅:⋅ By Walt Disney

Registered U. S. Patent Office

February 23, 1938. The first appearance in the daily strips of one of Donald's three nephews. Written by Bob Karp; drawn by Al Taliaferro.

DONALD DUCK ⋅:⋅ ⋅:⋅ ⋅:⋅ ⋅:⋅ ⋅:⋅ By Walt Disney

Registered U. S. Patent Office

April 26, 1938. Initial appearance of all three nephews. Written by Bob Karp; drawn by Al Taliaferro.

DONALD DUCK ⋅:⋅ ⋅:⋅ ⋅:⋅ ⋅:⋅ ⋅:⋅ ⋅:⋅ By Walt Disney

Registered U. S. Patent Office

September 26, 1938. The first appearance in the daily strips of Donald's three nephews by name: Huey, Dewey, and Louie. Written by Bob Karp; drawn by Al Taliaferro.

December 10, 1939. The first Sunday color page. Written and drawn by Karp and Taliaferro.

February 25, 1940. The first appearance of Huey, Dewey, and Louie in the Sunday papers. Written and drawn by Karp and Taliaferro.

November 4, 1940. The first appearance in the daily strips of Donald's girl friend, Daisy. Written and drawn by Karp and Taliaferro.

September 27, 1943. The first appearance of "Grandma" in the daily strips.

December 19, 1961. One of the first appearances in the daily strips of Professor Ludwig von Drake.

July 14, 1964. One of the first appearances of Uncle Scrooge McDuck in the daily strips. Written and drawn by Karp and Taliaferro.

January 24, 1960. Scrooge McDuck's first appearance in the Sunday papers—and in his gray smoking jacket. Written and drawn by Karp and Taliaferro.

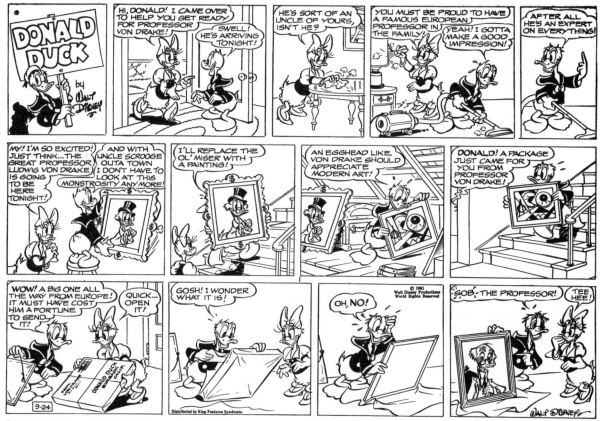

September 24, 1961. The first Sunday appearance of von Drake. Written and drawn by Karp and Taliaferro.

In the early 1930s, Disney had already entered the publishing world as part of the merchandising of Mickey. There were three series of *Mickey Mouse* magazines published, all of them compilations of miscellaneous articles, stories, poems, jokes, puzzles, and games. The first magazine was distributed through movie theaters and department stores selling Disney merchandise, the second through dairies. The third magazine, launched as "A Fun Book for Children to Read to Grown-Ups," went on sale at newsstands in 1935, but hard times and dwindling distribution ended it in October 1940.

Much of the problem lay in the fact that the comic book craze was growing. *Detective Comics*, the first comic book devoted to a single theme, had appeared in 1937, followed closely by *Superman, Doc Savage, Batman and Robin, Captain Marvel, Captain America*, and *Wonder Woman*. Readers, transported to new heights of fantasy by these comics, became hungry for more stories of wonder and adventure. For Disney to compete for attention, he had to offer more than games and puzzles.

Walt Disney's Comics and Stories were the solution; 252,000 copies of Volume 1, Number 1, were published by Dell in October 1940, with Donald Duck winking out from the cover. This was not the first time, however, that the Duck had posed as a cover boy. Donald had appeared in a number of comic books that collectors consider the first from Disney. In 1938, KK Publications produced a black-and-white Donald Duck comic book with cardboard covers (which some classify as a book rather than a comic); in 1940, Dell published a black-and-white comic book featuring Donald and, a year later, a black-and-white Donald Duck comic paint book. A few months before *Comics and Stories*, Donald appeared in Dell Color Comics, which featured a wide variety of characters, including Disney's. These early comics are very rare and valuable.

There was a problem with *Comics and Stories*—the material included in each issue consisted of reprints of comic strips and plots that had been taken from cartoons. Donald was being represented by the first-rate strips of Karp and Taliaferro, but those alone were not enough to establish a comic book kingdom. The Duck's original comic book started as an experiment.

In 1942 Disney story men Harry Reeves and Homer Brightman had plans for a full-length movie called *Donald Duck Finds Pirate Gold*. Because of the interruption of war work, the film was shelved and never produced. At Walt's suggestion, Duck unit men Jack Hannah and Carl Barks volunteered to take the story and turn it into a comic book in their spare time. Bob Karp broke the story down into panels for them and each man produced thirty-two of the sixty-four pages of the comic (Dell Four-Color Comics #9*) that now sells for as much as $1,800.

Carl Barks, who for years was known to comic book fans only as "The Good Artist."

This, then, was the beginning of Donald Duck in comic books. The list of his publications grew as rapidly as they could be produced. (A meticulous catalog of the regular comics, the giant-size comics, and giveaways can be found in Cecil Munsey's *Disneyana*.) Collecting Donald Duck comics is a lucrative hobby as well as a passion. According to the *Comic Book Price Guide #8*, in 1971 a complete mint run of Donald Duck comics was valued at $604. By 1977 it had increased to $7,892, making each $100 initially invested in 1971 worth over $1,300 six years later. Of the fifty most valuable comic books, nine are Donald Ducks.

Pirate Gold marked the beginning of Carl Barks's career as a comic book artist in 1942. Barks's Donald Duck comic books are the most sought after and highly valued. Prices for mint condition quoted according to *The Comic Book Price Guide #9 (1979)*.

Pirate Gold (1942), $1800.

For millions of Donald Duck fans, the greatest significance of *Pirate Gold* was the beginning of Carl Barks's career as a comic book artist. The Duck man who for years was only known as "The Good Artist," is now of such tremendous stature in the realm of comic books that fans venerate him as "The Comic Book King." There was even a special fan publication devoted to him—*The Barks Collector*.

The king's beginnings, like Donald's, of course, were humble. Barks was born on March 27, 1901, on a small grain ranch near Merrill, Oregon, and led an isolated rural life that included his being in a one-room schoolhouse until the end of eighth grade. Except for a few mail-order lessons, he never received any formal art training. He taught himself to do cartoon art while farmwork kept him from starving. In December, 1918, Barks left Oregon in search of a way to break into cartooning. He first went to San Francisco, where he found work in a printing office and made unsuccessful tries for jobs with local newspapers.

Several years later, Barks returned to Oregon and spent a summer as a logger. During the next six and a half years he worked hard in the railroad yards of Roseville, California, doing piecework riveting. "I always felt that cartooning would be an easier job than any of the other things that I worked at," Carl has said. And so all throughout his stints as a laborer, he submitted drawings and gags to various magazines and finally sold his first cartoon to a risqué Canadian humor publication called *The Calgary Eye-Opener*. After his material appeared there several more times, he quit the riveting gang without a second thought and continued to free-lance for the *Eye-Opener* until 1931. Next Barks was asked to join the staff as a full-time artist. He was in paradise. Not only had he achieved his dream of becoming a professional cartoonist, but during the Depression he was making a whopping $110 a month.

A few years later Barks heard of work at the Disney Studio. He had been following Mickey's adventures in the daily strips and, feeling certain that Disney would like his similar style, sent in some of his samples. His hunch proved correct and Barks was hired as an artist in 1935. Turning down a raise to stay at the *Eye-Opener,* he came to the Disney Studio at the salary of $20 a week.

Like everyone else, Barks started out as an in-betweener. His particular assignment was on the Duck cartoons. With his previous experience he found that he was better as a gag man than as an artist and transferred to the story department after only six months. For six and a half years he worked on continuity, brainstorming with the animators and roughing out the storyboards. Among his story credits are *Donald's Nephews, Self-Control, Donald's Better Self,* and *Mr. Duck Steps Out.* All the time he worked on stories, his artistry went undeveloped.

With the shift to the war films, Barks lost interest in his work in the Studio. Having decided to leave the smog-ridden surroundings of Los Angeles, he claims that he shut the door one Friday night and never came back. His plan was to move to San Jacinto to start a chicken ranch, but fate would not let him escape the Duck. A few months later he heard that Western Printing and Lithographing Company was looking for artists to provide original material for *Comics and Stories.* Rather than taking the time to create and develop his own comic book character, he decided to free-lance with the one he knew best— Donald.

The first comic was not entirely Barks's. Western sent him the script for a story that had Donald protecting his victory garden from some nasty crows, and Barks, the consummate story man, asked for permission to edit and correct plot errors. The Western people, located in Poughkeepsie, New York, allowed him to make the necessary changes, and were so impressed that they asked Barks to write and illustrate his own ten-page Donald Duck story. With that, he was off on a spectacular career that would take his imagination—and those of adult and child readers—where no comic book artist's had gone before.

***Mummy's Ring**
(1943), $1200.*

***Frozen Gold**
(1945), $600.*

I was a fizzle as a cowboy, a logger, a printing press feeder, a steelworker, a carpenter, an animator, a chicken grower, and a barfly. Perhaps that all helped in writing my stories of the ineptitudes of poor old Donald.

—Carl Barks

hatever the reason for his understanding of the Duck, Barks transformed Donald into a character of incredible substance, complexity, and range. In ten-page stories and thirty-two-page "one-shots" (books that only contained one story), he drew readers into Donald's unique world again and again, satisfying them with comedy, adventure, and subtle psychological dramas, yet leaving them eager for more. From the monthly *Comics and Stories* a reader felt that he could know but not entirely predict Donald, and that was much of the fun. After decades of such rich characterization and vast scope, Barks became the subject of intense and

Terror of the River (1946), $360.

Volcano Valley (1947), $240.

Ghost of the Grotto (1947), $210.

scholarly studies. Mike Barrier's "The Lord of Quackly Hall" (first published in *Funnyworld* in 1967) is both a loving, glowing tribute and a minutely detailed examination of the entire Barks cosmos—the definitive critical work to date. A lengthy interview with him was published by *Comic Book Art* in 1968, and articles continue to appear from time to time, such as "Carl Barks and the Donald Duck Gestalt" or the mock-serious "Donald Duck: An Interview" in a 1973 issue of *Radical America*. An excerpt from the latter: "Originally (because he was rumored to have leaked the names of strikers at Disney to HUAC) we had made no plans to interview Donald Duck whom we frankly considered to be representative of the worst petit bourgeois tendencies in American popular culture. . . ."

When he began to draw Donald, Barks was still under the influence of his Disney training. His early comics depended more on sight gags than dialogue, although later Barks's incisive and expressive words would help accomplish the transformation from one-dimensional squawking Duck to a full-dimensional talking (and therefore thinking) person. This is not to say that the Disney training was a drawback for Barks. He speaks gratefully of his years in the story department and his experience with Walt, acknowledging that it taught him how to condense and polish his stories to perfection.

While part of his technical expertise was derived from his animation work, there was a side to Barks's style that was wholly his own. More than any other comic artist, Barks did not condescend to his readers by offering pat story lines and moral simplicity. Although he believed that he was writing for twelve- to thirteen-year-olds, his subject matter, his vocabulary, and his satirical outlook indicate that he was writing for adults. In fact, most Barks collectors are well over thirteen. Children seem to prefer the superheroes, thinking that animal stories are babyish.

arks's Donald Duck stories can be divided into two categories by length and by approach. First were the monthly ten-pagers which usually portrayed Donald and the nephews at home in Duckburg. These stories abounded in comedy and satire while they focused on family conflicts, Donald's jobs, and everyday situations. They were the dramas that revealed Donald as Everyduck beset by the problems of raising a family, keeping a home, and staying in budget. Donald and his brood mirrored the reactions of real families—right down to name-calling, petty spats, and heartfelt fury.

Barks has admitted that he preferred doing the other type of stories—the twenty- to thirty-two-page one-shots which were first published irregularly and then on a bimonthly schedule in the early fifties. The one-shots opened up fantastic new vistas for Donald, his nephews, and the new supporting characters created by Barks. Freed from the limitations imposed by the technical range and expense of animation, they could travel at whim to faraway exotic lands and partake in costume productions as visually exciting and opulent as any grand opera production.

"Mummy's Ring"..."Voodoo Hoodoo"..."Land of the Totem Poles"..."Ancient Persia"..."Maharajah Donald"..."The Old Castle's Secret"..."Lost in the Andes.".... The titles alone suggest the sweep and enchantment of the adventure, and often Barks further enriched his epic stories by infusing them with the most fabulous and provocative myths in our lore. Over the years the Duck discovered the Fountain of Youth, the Philosopher's Stone, the unicorn, the legendary mines of King Solomon, the long-lost gold of the Mayas, the caves that hid the treasures of Ulysses and Circe, the Golden Fleece, and Atlantis. "As for my use of myths in the plots of my stories, the reason is laziness, admits Barks." "A myth gave me many plot gimmicks upon which to base the actions and motivations."

When it came to creating his own mythology, Barks was far from lazy. The Duck encountered many weird and wonderful characters on his travels—including the Gneezles (little goblins of the Everglades) and the Terries and the Firmies (whose underground earthshaking battles threatened Scrooge's money bin). Barks also evolved memorable Duck legends—Scrooge's lucky first dime, for instance.

The adventure stories were a brilliant synthesis of drama, suspense, and comedy character interplay. They had the power to involve the reader on several levels—emotional, intellectual, and fantasy. As each episode began, Donald and his nephews were home engaging in some mundane activity which encouraged the reader to identify with the Duck's situation. "The Gilded Man" begins with Donald working on his stamp collection; in "Land of the Totem Poles" he is reading the want ads in the newspaper; at other times, he overhears gossip in the streets of Duckburg, is reluctantly shoveling snow, working at a boring job (third assistant janitor), or taking in the city sights with Huey, Dewey, and Louie. With the initial identification with reality made, the identification with the ensuing fantasy becomes that much easier for the reader.

On many occasions Donald's call to adventure is provided by an outside source—Uncle Scrooge sending him to the ends of the world with an impossible request, such as a unicorn, or an Eskimo community asking that penicillin be flown in ("Frozen Gold"). At other times, the motivation is internal. In one instance, when Donald is working as a museum guard ("The Golden Helmet") we get a palpable sense of his middle-class ennui and his deeply felt longing to be a hero: "Those old Vikings fought walruses and whales and savage tribes, and I tell goggle-eyed nature boys where to find butterflies! Oh, that the race of men could sink so low!" says Donald, with a world-weary expression sure to break any heart. "I'm going up on deck of this old scow for a few minutes and *pretend* that I'm *a he-man*."

But before this story (and many others like it) is over,

Christmas on Bear Mountain (1947), $210—Uncle Scrooge's first appearance.

The Old Castle's Secret (1964), $180.

Sheriff of Bullet Valley (1948), $180.

Dangerous Disguise (1951), $66.

No Such Varmint (1951), $66.

Old California (1951), $75.

Donald does not have to pretend. Barks gave Donald the identity of hero; time and time again the Duck's impulsive nature led him to face the cruelest adversaries and the most threatening situations with determination and clear-headed courage. The appeal of Donald's Barks-rounded personality, though, was that even in the midst of showing virtue or valor, the dark side of his being was never totally eclipsed. When he finds the golden Viking Helmet, for instance, he is overcome by the greedy thrill of becoming King Donald, owner of North America, owner of everything, including the air! As in a Greek tragedy, Donald is inevitably punished for his hubris, but not as drastically as some tragic heroes. The last panel of the comic finds him back at the museum, excited by the prospect of guiding a patron to the embroidered lampshades.

In Barks's comic book stories, more than ever, Donald is a believable *human*. Barks deliberately blurred the bounds of his character by alternately referring to him as a person and as a duck. While Donald often talks about his feathers and his tail, one of the nephews, horrified that Scrooge might want Donald for his zoo, avows, "Unca Donald is not an animal!" One has only to examine his speeches to see that this is true. Donald can articulate all his emotions, hopes, and dreams, his fears, his jealousies, his inadequacies ("And worst of all, I heard the kids say they were going to spend five dollars for my present. I feel cheap!"). At times, as all of us feel, words are not enough. He can still bash his head against the wall in utter rage and frustration.

Donald is also illuminated in his relationships to other characters. His dealings with his nephews reveal him as a typical parent unable to conceal his ambivalence toward his kids. All in the space of one story he can range from calling them numbskulls to feeling unabashed joy at seeing them alive. He can argue with them and deliberately hurt their feelings—and then feel genuine anguish.

Barks had inherited the nephews from the movies, and while he wasn't able to give each a separate identity, he did give them new status and significance collectively. Huey, Dewey, and Louie were no longer cute little tricksters—they grew to be heroic personalities, wise beyond their years.

But in one sense, the nephews always remained children. Dependent on Donald for food and shelter, they had to follow orders, accept punishment, and go where he went. Yet by talking back and criticizing, they openly rebelled against Donald to work out their conflicts (an act usually forbidden to children), and for this young readers were powerfully drawn to them.

Barks took the appeal one step further by feeding a child's fantasy of overcoming his parent. The nephews possessed an intelligence that was far superior to Donald's; winning out over him, they prove that *they* were the grown-ups of the stories—a much-wished-for role reversal. The nephews' intelligence was not always used for Donald's destruction, however. Mike Barrier has pointed out the "rescue" theme, showing how they turned their skills and resourcefulness against the enemy to save Donald's life. In "Voodoo Hoodoo," for example, they buy Donald's freedom from a witch doctor; in "Adventure Down Under," they release him from the terrifying clutches of Australian bushmen. For the younger reader, these rescues take on great emotional impact, since they reemphasize the parent/child role reversal and heighten the joy of the fantasy.

In addition to their maturity, Huey, Dewey, and Louie could be admired for their sense of values. The story "A Christmas for Shacktown" showed them at their moral best—concerned, compassionate, altruistic—the epitome of the spirit of Christmas. Walking through the slums near Duckburg, they confess to feeling like "pigs." Barks's touching, sentimental story follows their efforts to raise money for the orphans who don't have toys or a Christmas turkey.

While the nephews' compassion, courage, and ingenuity were portrayed as innate qualities, their encyclopedic knowledge came from a brilliant device by Barks—their association with what is perhaps the best-known club in all of comic books, the Junior Woodchucks. Guided by a handbook that held a reservoir of "inexhaustible knowledge," the nephews had a valid reason for knowing anything and everything and being able to squeeze out of any tight spot. Many times Donald's fortune changed for the better when a nephew announced, "It says in the Junior Woodchuck guide. . . ."

The Junior Woodchucks, who first appeared in the February, 1951 *Walt Disney's Comics and Stories*, were created by Barks as a gentle parody of the Boy Scouts and had a structural organization going up to and beyond "International Twelve-Star Admiral and Deputy Custodian of the Fountain of Inexhaustible Knowledge." Junior Woodchucks could also aspire to "Omnipotent Overseers of the Quest for Unsurpassable Excellence." One of their leaders was B.E.L.L.E.R.I.N.G. B.U.L.L.N.E.C.K.—"Bellicose Expecter of Limitless Lionization, Esteem, Reverence and Indefatigable, Never-dying Gung-ho, as well as Bedeviller of Unskillful, Lunkheaded Lallygaggers, and Nemesis of Extemporizing Campground Know-nothings." The Junior Woodchucks became a subject of fascination all over the world. An actual guide has been written and published in Italy, France, Norway, Denmark, Sweden, Germany, Mexico, and Brazil. The limited English edition was distributed through a premium deal in the United States.

s Donald and his nephews became allies in adventure, Barks needed other characters to play against the Duck. In 1948 Gladstone Gander ambled along—a wavy-haired duck who dressed in flashy clothes and spats—just the right image for a character described as a "loafer, bum, chiseler and connoisseur of the fast buck." Soon Barks gave Gladstone his most memorable and annoying characteristic—unheard-of good luck—which became the bane of Donald's existence. It

A Christmas for Shacktown (1952), $54.

The Golden Helmet (1952), $48.

The Gilded Man (1952), $48.

Trick or Treat (1953), $45.

Walt Disney's Christmas Parade (1949), $90.

Walt Disney's Christmas Parade (1950), $48.

was a fact that wherever he went Gladstone stumbled over diamonds and rubies, ten-dollar bills floated into his hands, and wallets appeared at his feet. When he tried to augment his luck by working at it (both cheating and wishing were forms of work)—something was bound to go wrong. As a gag Gladstone was funny, but as a character he was insufferable—boastful, condescending, and rigid. Barks was aware of his limitations and did not use him often.

Another supporting character was Gyro Gearloose, a red-haired, bespectacled, four-foot-tall chicken, who added a touch of fascination to Donald Duck comics with his weird and amazing inventions. He dreamed up "think boxes" that taught animals to speak, trained worms, built a mind-reading robot, a mechanical firefly tracker, and scores of absurd contraptions that surprised Gyro and Donald by malfunctioning. Somewhat of an absentminded professor, Gyro played his part for laughs, but from time to time came out with a noteworthy comment. ("Nobody can make a machine so smart that some jerk won't be too dumb to run it.") Unexpectedly, Gyro found an appreciative audience. From 1959 to 1962 Dell published five Gyro Gearloose comic books, four of which were written and illustrated by Barks.

The regular female character in Donald Duck's comic book world was his longtime steady, Daisy. Barks didn't use her very often and when he did she came across as mean, demanding, and even fearsome. Barks fan Barbara E. Boatner has pointed out that "Barks had very little use for female characters. . .[he used Daisy] a bit like Keaton did heroines: she was there to move along a piece of action and was then retired from the field." Starting in 1954, there was a series of one-shots titled *Daisy Duck's Diary*. Barks drew two of them, but had nothing to do with the stories.

Carl Barks's greatest and best-loved creation was Uncle Scrooge McDuck. In a span of three decades he grew to such importance that he earned an entire page in *The People's Almanac* as "Famous Nonperson"—an honor shared by Sherlock Holmes. First seen in the 1947 story "Christmas on Bear Mountain," the wealthy old duck was never intended to become such a big part of Donald's life. Barks recalls, "I just needed a rich uncle for the story that I was going to do. I thought of this situation of Donald getting involved with a bear up in the mountains. Somebody had to own this cabin he was going to, so I invented Uncle Scrooge as the owner."

In the beginning Scrooge was *not* the world's wealthiest duck. He was a decrepit, despicable old miser who grumbled and "bah-humbugged!" about Christmas as intensely as his Dickensian prototype: "That silly season when everybody loves everybody else!. . . Everybody hates me, and I hate everybody!"

Little by little, Scrooge evolved into a character with depth,

acquiring new personality traits with each new story. His
fortune, too, continued to grow until in 1948 he was described
as "the richest old coot in the world." (Trying to keep track of
how much money Scrooge has amassed is one of the great
joys—and biggest difficulties—of reading *Uncle $crooge*. At
various times McDuck himself cites different figures: eleven
octillion; 250 umtillion and sixteen cents; five billion quintuptil-
lion umtuplatillion multuplatillion impossibidillion fantasticatril-
lion; uncountabillions and sixteen cents. A scientist at the
Pasadena Jet Propulsion laboratory estimated the fortune at six
septillion dollars. According to this author's calculations, the
figure is $315,567,360,000,000,000 . . . plus 10 cents for his lucky
dime. I base my calculations on a line from "The Magic
Hourglass": "Losing a billion dollars a minute, I'll be broke in 600
years," says Scrooge.

Barks scholars agree that in "Letter to Santa," Scrooge
assumed his "classic" identity both physically and morally. He
began wearing the old red broadcloth coat he bought in
Scotland in 1902, sporting a black silk top hat, and carrying a
cane. His preoccupation with money has transformed him into a
vain, selfish, and belligerent character. In fact, he's lost all sight
of what money is for and turned it into an end in itself. As he
wallows in his coins he exults, "People that spend money are
saps . . . they don't know how to enjoy it."

Scrooge *was* hateful at first, but Barks took a liking to him
and softened his character, most notably in the first *Uncle
$crooge* comic book published in 1952—"Only a Poor Man."
This funny and sad story reveals all that was *ever* to be revealed
about Scrooge. Barks probes all the effects of having money,
leaving us to hate, admire, and pity Scrooge all at the same
time . . . and as always, to fantasize about possessing his wealth.

As the story opens, Scrooge, seized by an attack of money
lust, is taking his daily money swim and glorifying his favorite
pleasures: "I like to dive around in it like a porpoise! And burrow
through it like a gopher! And toss it up and let it hit me on the
head!" He repeats this refrain several times during the story; it is
a cherished litany to him. Scrooge then attempts to explain to
Donald what a joy and comfort money is, but is distracted by
immediate threats to his fortune—a rat that can chew up
greenbacks, moths that could eat holes in them, a spider that
could short-circuit a burglar alarm, and worst of all, the terrible
Beagle Boys. Scrooge reacts with panic and tears.

At first we see Scrooge's annoyance, fear, and utter dread
as neurotic and laughable, until we learn that the old duck has a
sentimental connection to each and every coin in the three
cubic acres of his money bin. "All this money *means* something
to me! Every coin in here has a story!" He proceeds to tell how
he made it big in the Klondike being "tougher than the toughies
and smarter than the smarties. And I made it square!" Which is
more than you can say for a lot of America's millionaires.
Scrooge isn't so bad after all, we think.

**The Golden
Christmas Tree
(1948), $105.**

**Lost in the Andes
(1949), $120.**

**Voodoo Hoodoo
(1949), $90.**

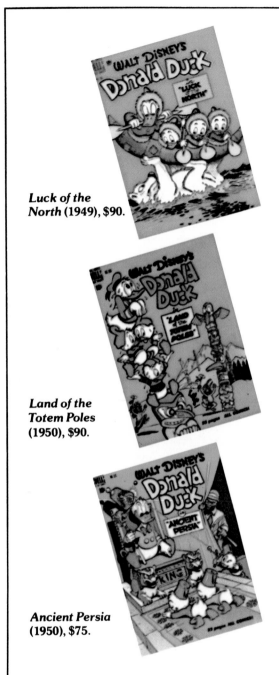

Luck of the North (1949), $90.

Land of the Totem Poles (1950), $90.

Ancient Persia (1950), $75.

As Scrooge summons up his courage to outsmart the Beagle Boys, a sleazy gang of ex-cons as obsessed with Scrooge's fortune as he was, he alternates between a touching vulnerability ("Don't leave me, boys...help me save my money") and the cold-hearted miserliness that makes him reluctant to pay his relatives for their help.

The comment in this story is provided by Donald, who has always shown great insight about the troubles that money brings Scrooge. "You may not know it, Uncle Scrooge, but your billions are a pain in the neck! You're only a poor old man!" But rather than ending the story on this dreary, moralistic note, Barks lets Scrooge redeem himself—and therefore triumph—by showing that he is self-aware and true to himself: "Bah! Kid talk! No man is poor who can do what he likes to do once in a while.... And I like to dive around in my money like a porpoise...." Twist endings such as this were a popular staple of Barks's stories.

With "Only a Poor Man," Scrooge had finally become a sympathetic character, but not for a moment did he lose the greedy impulse that could obviate his humanity. Once again at his most evil in "The Magic Hourglass," he finds Donald and the nephews dying of thirst in the desert. "I intended to be generous with them but—when I have somebody at my mercy, I just can't help myself, I drive a hard bargain." He trades them his water bag for their hourglass, only to offer them a billion dollars *and* the hourglass when he is dying of thirst a little later. Donald proves that he is the bigger man of the two by *giving* Scrooge a drink of water. He also forces him to take back his gift of a rotten fishing boat, and a chastised Scrooge admits, "Those ducks drive a hard bargain."

In spite of temporary repentance for his stinginess, Scrooge continued to exploit his family in an appalling manner. He gave them worthless gifts and refused to pay for their services. A phone call from him could turn Donald into a simpering yes-man, his commands sent him off on any number of dangerous missions. In "Voodoo Hoodoo," because of a case of mistaken identity, Scrooge even let Donald take his place as the object of a horrible curse. By then Donald was at the point where he could express his anger at Scrooge—he firmly kicked him in his tailfeathers.

No matter how many times his family helped or rescued him in Barks's stories, the most important thing in Scrooge's life continued to be his money bin. Over and over it was threatened by floods, earthquakes, lightning, and the Beagle Boys. But Barks felt unable to use the Beagle Boys too often, so he created the frightening sorceress, Magica de Spell, whose villainous aim was to spirit away Scrooge's lucky dime. To that end she cast terrifying spells, brewed potions concocted by Circe, and scared the living daylights out of Scrooge. Barks liked Magica because she was capable of so many things. He also admitted that "she brought in an opportunity to kid this

Superman stuff—the superwitches and the weird things that you find in some of the other comics."

Kidding, in fact, was as much a part of Barks's art as the complexity of his characters and his flawless narrative structures. One aspect of his humor was rampant punning; the names of minor characters offered a rich opportunity.

There was Petrolio de Vaselino, the South American oil tycoon; King Nevvawazza, imperial potentate of Itsa Faka; he also created Don Porko de Lardo, Rockjaw Bumrisk, Professors Utterbunk, Batty, and Pulpheart Clabberhead (a takeoff on Dr. Spock), and the mysterious Arabs, Prince Cad Ali Cad, Hassen Ben Jailed, and Mustapha Handout. More serious kidding took the form of satire. Barks poked fun at intellectuals, federal agents, science fiction, health foods, and took some deep stabs at lawyers. In "The Golden Helmet" he reduced legal language to so much double-talk ("Hocus, Locus, Jocus!. . . which means, to the landlord belong the doorknobs!") and went on to expose the true nature of the law. In one scene Donald says to Lawyer Sharky, "I wonder if there isn't such a thing as punishment!" "Not with a smart lawyer," is the character's (we can infer Barks's) cynical reply. Humor like this explains why Barks has such appeal to older readers.

No aspect of Barks's art has gone unpraised. His fans often mention his knack for rendering motion, his sweeping panoramas in the adventure stories, and his great attention to comic detail—such as a painting of an egg entitled "Mom," goldfish that wore diving helmets, "Godiva's laundry bag" in a museum, signs pointing opposite ways to darkest and lightest Africa. . .the list is endless. Most of all they point to the vivid realism that Barks wove into his stories, even in the middle of the most fantastic plots. To achieve such true-to-life effects, Barks drew all of his references—locales, costumes, customs, scientific facts—from *National Geographic* and the *Encyclopaedia Britannica*. He was not the world traveler that many supposed him to be.

Just how realistic the comics were is best illustrated by the true story of Karl Kroyer, a Danish inventor. Kroyer once salvaged a sunken ship from Kuwait harbor in a tenth of the usual time by pumping expandable polystyrene foam into its hull. When he went to register the technique he was denied a patent because the process had already been described in print. *Walt Disney's Comics and Stories #104*, a Barks story, showed Donald and the kids raising a ship with ping-pong balls.

To produce a ten-page story with eight panels to a page it took Barks four days of writing and six days of drawing. (After 1952 his wife, Gare, helped with the blacking, lettering, and some of the background detail work.) His top scale during his career was $34 per page for art, $11.50 for script. In 1960, his most prolific year, he produced 358 pages of art, 249 pages of script, 15 covers, and 4 cover gags.

The Pixilated Parrot (1950), $75.

The Magic Hourglass (1950), $75.

Big Top Bedlam (1950), $66.

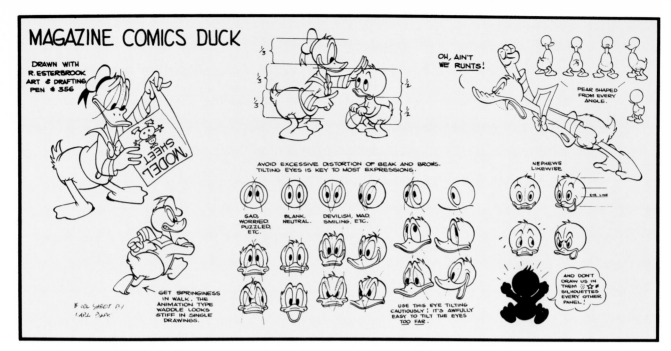

A model sheet by Carl Barks illustrates his special brand of humor.

Barks's drawing technique itself was held in awe. Michael McGuire's critical assessment of it in the *Daily Iowan* stressed, among other skills, Barks's firm grip on "the plastics of the medium":

Barks used the comic page for some of the cleverest cutting and shaping of images in the comic narrative, translating the tension between characters and situations into the locking of the panels. Typical is Barks' use of conflict in his montage (aiming the directions of actions in adjacent frames into one another) and his tendency to distort the shapes of his frames to achieve some of his effects. He frequently used a kind of Caligarian geometrical framing to capture the tumultuous struggles between Donald Duck and his feisty Uncle Scrooge....

And Barks had always considered himself a hack.

In 1966, with some 450 comics to his credit (not all Donald Duck or Scrooge), Barks retired from Western Printing to live a less-pressured life in Temecula, California. "The Good Artist" had finally lost interest in ducks and began to do paintings of little girls, landscapes, and South California Indians. His fans would not stand for his retirement, though. So Barks wrote to the Disney Studio and obtained permission to try his paintbrush at the ducks. From 1971 until 1976, Barks did more than 100 large oils depicting scenes from his classic comics. He sold the first one to a fan for $50; the last, a Bicentennial parade in Duckburg, was auctioned in 1977 for $6,400.

Only in the past decade has Carl Barks come to be recognized for his work. By now he has been honored with a Duckster from the Disney Studio, the 1970 Shazam Award for Best Writer, Humor Division, from the Academy of Comic Books, and the adulation of millions.

The Carl Barks Gallery

Donald and the nephews find their way into Scrooge's vault in "Hands Off My Playthings," 1975.

Scrooge's money bin is invaded by a "Visitor from Underground," 1973.

A situation that could only happen to Scrooge McDuck. One of several small-size paintings done in 1975.

Donald shoots it up in "The Sheriff of Bullet Valley" (1948).

Christmas brings goodwill to everyone but Scrooge McDuck in "Season to Be Jolly," 1974.

True to form, Uncle Scrooge finds a way to turn a profit even at Christmastime.

Donald and his nephews match wits with Azure Blue and Sharky in the quest for
"The Golden Helmet," 1952.

Donald and the TV Years

Many a lighthearted moment was provided when Donald entered Walt's office on "Walt Disney Presents."

fter his blaze of glory during the war era, Donald, like millions of other Americans, longed to return to his civilian role. As so many GI's did, he found that the home front had changed in his absence. In his case, the market for animated shorts was rapidly shrinking—so much so that only a few years later, in 1953, Mickey Mouse became the first to be retired from the Disney cartoon industry. Donald, still exceedingly more popular than the Mouse, was allowed to continue to act in new shorts until 1956, and for a few years after that in lengthier (approximately twenty minutes) "specials" released to movie theaters.

While Donald's film contract was running out, a new development was taking place in the entertainment world. Television—still a relatively new invention—was becoming a national pastime, with the promise of attracting bigger audiences than ever thought possible. Although most producers were predicting that TV would mean the demise of movies, Disney sensed opportunity in the airwaves. With characteristic foresight, he had retained the rights to all of his cartoons in anticipation of the day that television would become a reality.

After airing several Christmas specials starting in 1950, Disney introduced the nation to this magic kingdom. "Disneyland" premiered on ABC-TV on Wednesday evening, October 27, 1954, to transport viewers to Fantasyland, Adventureland, Frontierland, or Tomorrowland for an hour each week. As with the shorts and features, Walt insisted on quality in his variety show. To that end, he once again supervised every step of production and, as usual, his work paid off. From the beginning, "Disneyland" earned high Nielsen ratings. Now having completed its twenty-fifth consecutive season in prime time as "The Wonderful World of Disney," no other show in television history has matched its record.

Cartoons, of course, were always an integral part of the show. Disney developed a format for showcasing vintage shorts by unifying them into one story with the addition of new footage. "Kids Is Kids," for instance, had Ludwig von Drake pontificating on child psychology in between six Donald Duck cartoons featuring Huey, Dewey, and Louie.

Donald made his TV debut in the fourth installment of "Disneyland," *The Donald Duck Story.* It consisted of a few classic Duck cartoons linked by Walt's narration and banter with an animated Donald. Scenes in Walt's office were always a high point of "Disneyland." Disney was a warm, charming host—he was even nominated for a 1955 Emmy as "Most Outstanding New Personality." As the show opens Walt describes to the audience the life story of "the Gable of our stable," while Donald is impatiently waiting outside his office, eager but nervous to make his television debut. One especially funny sequence has Walt describing how the animators tried to find the right animal for Ducky Nash's voice. We then witness a horse, a bear, a cow, a zebra, and other unlikely animals speaking in the famous quacks. In this scene, Walt took liberties with history, but at the time there were probably few who realized or cared about it.

When at last Walt ushers the Duck into his office, Donald delivers some quick spoofs of standard TV fare—he plays a Bogie-like detective, cowboy, quiz show host—and the next scene finds Walt frantically taking phone calls from viewers complaining that they can't understand a word Donald is saying! Disney quickly remedies the situation by adding subtitles to the show, but Donald is absolutely distraught and fears that he's washed up on TV. "Be yourself," advises Walt. And Donald listened. He went on to star in many more shows, *Donald's Silver Anniversary, A Day in the Life of Donald Duck, At Home with Donald Duck, Your Host, Donald Duck,* and *Donald's Award* among them. For the 1958 season, the show was retitled "Walt Disney Presents," and two years later it moved to Sunday nights.

In 1960. . .

4 Full Hour **DONALD DUCK TV** Shows ON "WALT DISNEY PRESENTS" between February and September.

60 solid minutes of DONALD DUCK cartoons reaching 35,000,000 viewers per show

or

total cumulative audience of 140,000,000

Donald's success on television was as great as his career in film.

One of Donald's proudest moments came on March 11, 1960, when Jiminy Cricket hosted *This is Your Life, Donald Duck*. Not only was Donald nostalgically reunited with the entire Disney gang from Mickey to Snow White to Johnny Appleseed, but his whole crazy life flashed before his and the audience's eyes—childhood, army days, first job, introduction to show business, and his romance with Daisy.

On September 24, 1961, viewers tuning into NBC at 7:30 P.M. might have been startled to see the NBC peacock out of his majestic station identification pose and angrily having his feathers ruffled by a strange, bespectacled duck speaking with an Austrian accent. This comic scene marked the debut of "Walt Disney's Wonderful World of Color" and introduced to millions the newest Disney duck, wacky but erudite Professor Ludwig von Drake—Donald's uncle, for purposes of identification.

Ludwig von Drake served two purposes on the "Wonderful World of Color." First, he was a compelling new character who

Above and opposite: Donald was both bemused and disgruntled when his whole life flashed before him in *This Is Your Life, Donald Duck* (1960).

Overleaf: Donald's Uncle Ludwig was first introduced on television amid a flurry of feathers with the NBC peacock.

In *Fly with Von Drake* (1963), the mad professor gets even madder.

enlivened a format that was already seven years old. Second, he was a teacher who could educate children while he entertained them. He had just the right personality blend of authority (he *was* a professor), enthusiasm, and antic behavior. Over the years, he lectured on a great variety of fascinating subjects— Spain, Alaska, outer space, physical fitness, the truth about Mother Goose, popular music. *Fly with Von Drake* gave the already lofty duck license to become ever loftier, and included scenes from one of the biggest Disney war efforts, *Victory Through Air Power*.

   Ludwig von Drake's ascendancy did not mean that Donald was out of the picture. Donald appeared on the very first show in one of his several featurettes. The name of the show was *Donald in Mathmagic Land*. A marvelously entertaining survey of mathematical principles, it presents Donald on safari in a strange, confusing, and foreboding forest of numbers (where the trees literally have square roots!), then being guided through the land by the Spirit of Adventure. Next Donald is transported back to the Greece of Pythagoras to learn about the magic properties of the pentagram, the golden rectangle, the spiral, and the mathematics of music. With a leap forward in time, the

Spirit explains how math relates to sports and games like chess and billiards. Throughout, the action is funny and lively, the animation stunning, and the information fascinating. Even to an adult who already understands right angles and harmonics, a journey through Mathmagic land is fun.

Another one of the late 1950s specials was *Scrooge McDuck and Money*. In his first and only venture into the motion picture world, Scrooge was called upon to play the role that von Drake usually played on television. Fittingly enough, there was no one better to teach viewers about the mysteries of big bucks and big business. Scrooge, talking with a Scottish accent and infinitely more benevolent than he appeared in his comics, explains to Huey, Dewey, and Louie how money has to "travel for its health" and, before advising them to invest the $1.95 from their piggy bank, details the problems of inflation, budgeting, checks, and banks. In this episode Scrooge as a teacher was adequate; however, as a character he paled in comparison to his other self. Without his malice and greed, there was nothing very striking about the fantasticatrillionaire duck. Back he went to the comic books, where he was better able to lust after his gold.

Uncle Scrooge teaches Huey, Dewey, and Louie the value of a buck in *Scrooge McDuck and Money* (1967).

Overleaf: **Donald discovers the wonders of mathematics in *Donald in Mathmagic Land* (1961), where he's guided by the Spirit of Adventure. Notice that the trees have square roots.**

Donald gets all tied up in his work in *How to Have an Accident at Work* (1959).

Donald and his nephews portray "dirty ducks" in *The Litterbug* (1961).

CHRISTMAS
GREETINGS

**Much to Donald's dismay, his nephews
became avid Mickey Mouse Club fans.**

In the meantime, Donald was being kept busy with
special projects. He illustrated the history of the wheel,
showed how to have an accident at work and at home,
and played a most annoying litterbug. In the sixties he
also appeared in several of Disney's highly praised
industrial films.

For the American Iron and Steel Institute he explained
"Steel and America" and taught millions of schoolchildren about
"Donald's Fire Survival Plan." Then, too, there were his daily
appearances on the Mickey Mouse Club, where no other
character could have made such a memorable smash hit with
the gang in the show's opening sequence. Nor would any other
character but Donald have had the audacity to break into
Mickey's song and sing his own praises (Remember? "Mickey
Mouse...DONALD DUCK! Mickey Mouse...DONALD
DUCK!"). Donald's behavior in the latter case was especially

From Walt Disney's T.V. Series "MICKEY MOUSE CLUB"

DONALD DUCK SONG

**Words and Music by
OLIVER WALLACE**

Who's got the sweet-est dis-po si-tion hm? one guess guess who?

— Who nev-er nev-er starts an ar-gu-ment__ hm

Who nev-er shows a bit of temp-er — 'ment___

Who's nev-er wrong but al-ways right__ oh yeah Who'd nev-er dream of

start-ing a fight ___ Who's gets stuck ___ with

all the bad luck _ no one __ but Don-ald Duck.

objectionable because his own song was sung on the Mickey Mouse Club. (The snappy little tune that had originally prefaced later Duck cartoons was written and composed by Oliver Wallace.) Nevertheless, it was overshadowed by the rousing Mickey Mouse Club theme ("Who's the leader of the club...") that went on to become the national anthem of junior America. When the New Mickey Mouse Club went on the air early in 1977, Donald was called back to repeat his role in the opening sequence (now revamped to a disco beat) and occasionally could be seen on the show in one of his classics.

ith his performing years over, Donald took up residence in Disneyland and Walt Disney World, strolling around with Mickey and Goofy, greeting young visitors and taking part in Audio-Animatronics shows. On occasion he took to the road in such gala productions as "Disney on Parade" and "Disney on Ice"; for a few years he floated above the streets of New York on Thanksgiving Day as a giant balloon in Macy's parade. The end of Donald Duck's active movie career left the already ailing cartoon industry without one of its brightest attractions. But for the world at large, the legend would continue.

Donald and Mickey in their current roles as official greeters at Disneyland and Walt Disney World.

No Mickey Mouse Club was complete without Donald's antics. His role in the opening of the show has become classic.

No Mickey Mouse Club was complete without Donald's antics. His role in the opening of the show has become classic.

Donald on the International Scene

Italians know Donald as Paperino.

Uncle Scrooge is appropriately known as Tío Rico (Uncle Rich) in Spain.

I t's Donald—Duck!" became the rallying cry heard in theaters around the world, for soon after becoming a domestic sensation, the Duck was widely exported overseas. From Europe to the Far East, moviegoers discovered that Donald, though American by birth, was universal in nature. He was quickly and lovingly adopted by people of all nations. Recognizing the Duck's contribution to world politics—and ignoring the fact that he is basically such an ornery fellow—Dr. Frank Monaghan of Yale University presented Donald with a D.I.F. (Doctor of International Friendship) in 1939. Donald himself appeared at the ceremony, resplendent in his academic robes and mortarboard.

Over the next forty years, Donald's status in all four corners of the earth was to grow and grow, perhaps even surpassing his popularity in the United States. Today his movies are seen in more than 76 countries, his daily strips appear in 100 foreign newspapers, his comic books are sold in 47 nations, and he is seen on television in 29 lands. Furthermore, Duck merchandise is just as popular with children overseas as it is with American kids. Donald Duck, in his identity as an international superstar, is a figure who is never out of his element—even when the waters are foreign.

In Italy he is known as Paperino. There he struts and quacks his way through his *disavventure* in comics, films, and daily strips and has been the subject of numerous special books. He is also well represented in character merchandise, gracing everything from ceramic wall and floor tiles to silver-plated flatware, playing cards, and commemorative coins made in gold, silver, and bronze. Perhaps the Italians like Donald so much because of his personality. After all, the Duck is fiery, hot-blooded, and very demonstrative when he speaks.

In France, too, Donald Duck is a national hero. He appears to his millions of fans and *amis* as a wonderfully expressive, salty, and typical French character. In comics and books, his squawks translate to "*groump!*" or "*Zut!*" and his complaints to "*Malheur!*" (loosely translated as "Nuts," literally as "Un-happiness!"). And he infuses his cursing with a Gallic eloquence (something that Donald could never get away with in America), muttering, "*Sacre nom d'une pipe!*" or yelling, "*Allez au diable! Laissez moi passer!*" ("Go to the devil! Let me pass!") Whether in France Donald is more of a lover is not well documented. At least in one instance, he prefers adventure with L'oncle Picsou (Uncle Scrooge) to a date with la belle Daisy.

In Spain and Mexico Donald can be found as an appropriately hot-tempered señor starring in such adventures as *Donald Furioso*. In Brazil, as Pato Donald, he is a favorite along with his nephews Huguinho, Zezinho, and Luisinho. Donald has also ventured to such faraway places as Japan, China, Malaysia, and Egypt. His presence in the Republic of San Marino made such a strong impression that in December, 1970 the tiny nation issued a special Donald Duck stamp. (Just his luck—Donald gets licked again!)

Indicative of Donald's immense popularity in Western Europe are well-established fan clubs with large and serious memberships. Although the Duck never had an organized fan club here—a glaring anomaly for a true-blue Hollywood star!—he enjoys the adulation due a screen idol in Amsterdam, Norway, and especially in West Germany.

In 1977, a twenty-seven-year-old meteorologist named Hans von Storch founded the German Society for the Promotion of Noncommercial Donaldism. "We have banded together to study the history and meaning of this world-famous all-too-human cartoon character," he explained to the press. He and fellow Duckophiles, who concentrate their attentions on Donald Duck comic books, are vehemently opposed to Donaldism for profit—that is, dealers who speculate in rare copies of comics, driving the prices beyond the reach of the majority of fans. The club, based in Hamburg, has a song ("When I Lie in My Coffin," a ditty that Donald sang many years ago), a constitution, a newsletter, a character merchandise museum, and even a long-term goal—the establishment of a Donald Duck chair at the University of Hamburg. In the meantime, the group has begun to delve into the many mysteries of Donald's comic book universe as created by their hero—and the final arbiter in Duck matters—Carl Barks. Among its first findings were the length of a Duck mile (44 centimeters or 17 inches, calculated from the length of a step taken by a 2-foot-tall duck) and the subsequent pinpointing of Duckburg's location on an island in the Atlantic Ocean near Washington, D.C. (A countertheory also substantiated by Barks's evidence places Duckburg on the California coast.) Still on the agenda are general Duck genealogy, crime in Duckburg, deciding whether Donald has teeth, and looking into the matter of Scrooge's apparent tax evasion. To belong to the German Society, it is necessary to have expert knowledge of every Donald comic ever published. The constitution states, however, that "complete possession of one's faculties is *not* necessary for membership."

Moving north, the passion for Donald does not cool. As Kalle Anka, he appears in many Swedish comics and books; as Anders And, he pops up in Denmark and urges children to join his book club.

As Donald Duck approaches 50, he retains his reputation as one of Hollywood's greatest film stars, but it is startling to realize that he has not made a cartoon for 18 years. Is Donald in danger of fading into oblivion? Is his future to be the object of worship only by weird comic-book collectors and fanatical film cults? Even now there are children who know of Donald from the cartoons they've seen on TV, but they hardly consider him the movie idol he once was. When asked what they thought of Donald Duck, children aged ten and under gave

Herr Donald Duck, and his three nephews, Tick, Trick, and Track.

The French version of the *Junior Woodchucks' Guide*.

In Finland, Donald is known as Kalle Anka.

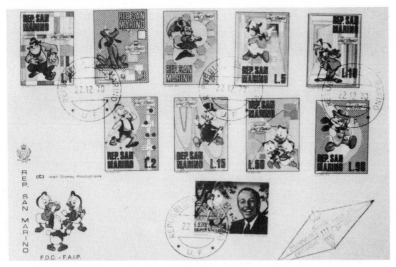

a variety of opinions, none of them particularly passionate, some of them downright indifferent: "He's good"..."He's a clown"..."Better than Mickey Mouse"..."Too crabby"..."A quacky legend in his own time"..."He talks like a frog," said one 7-year-old.

What *will* become of Donald Duck?

As long as he stays in the public eye with recycled cartoons, funny new comic strips and fun-filled toys and merchandise, Donald will not be forgotten by anyone. Year in and year out, he remains a contemporary, relevant, and wholly satisfying character. Children—even if they can't express their feelings—are always fascinated by his quirks as well as his quacks; adults will always have a soft spot in their hearts for the Duck who enlivened so many fondly remembered Saturday afternoons.

Like Mickey, Donald has stood up well to the test of time. His performances both technically and artistically far outshine those by the new animated characters on Saturday morning television. The gags are still the funniest and most intricate; the humor still fresh; the art more dazzling than ever.

In the past few years, there has been a remarkable resurgence of interest in old comic-book characters—from Wonder Woman, Spider-Man, and The Incredible Hulk on television to the making of the full-length movie of Superman. It can only be a matter of time before Donald, too, bows to the time-honored tradition of the Hollywood comeback...before there are gala premieres...before there are Donald Duck TV specials...before there are week-long Donald Duck film festivals and more.

The talent needed to bring Donald back to the screen is not lacking. A new generation of Disney animators could make the Duck as wild, brilliant, and distinctive as he was in his heyday. The world would certainly welcome a new Donald Duck. But if he never materializes, the old one—that familiar hothead, loudmouth, and sore loser—that beloved entertainer, hero, and human being—will do just fine.

Filmography

CARTOONS

From 1937 to 1961, 128 cartoons were released in the Donald Duck series. Also noted here are Donald's appearances in other Disney series.

* Academy Award nomination for Best Short

** Academy Award winner for Best Short

1934

The Wise Little Hen (Silly Symphony)
Donald and Peter Pig refuse to help the Hen plant or harvest her corn, but are eager to eat it. Hen tricks them; they get castor oil for a meal.

Orphan's Benefit (Mickey Mouse cartoon)
In Mickey's show Donald recites poetry before an audience of merciless child hecklers.

The Dognapper (MM cartoon)
Mickey and Donald rescue Minnie's Pekingese from the evil clutches of Pegleg Pete.

1935

The Band Concert (MM cartoon, 1st in Technicolor)
A park concert turns into a musical feud between Maestro Mickey and Donald, a peanut vendor. Climaxes with the *William Tell Overture* and a cyclone.

Mickey's Service Station (MM cartoon)
Mickey, Donald, and Goofy dismantle Pete's squeaking car and find a cricket.

Mickey's Fire Brigade (MM cartoon)
Mickey, Donald, and Goofy save Clarabelle from fire but wind up in the bathtub with her.

On Ice (MM cartoon)
Donald's skating and fishing antics with Mickey, Goofy, and Pluto.

1936

Mickey's Polo Team (MM cartoon)
Donald joins Mickey's team against film star opponents.

Orphan's Picnic ((MM cartoon)
On a picnic, Mickey and Donald are tormented by orphans and bees.

Mickey's Grand Opera (MM cartoon)
Donald and Clara Cluck harmonize in an aria from *Rigoletto*.

Moving Day (MM cartoon)
Pete gets a bang out of evicting Mickey and Donald; the gas-filled house blows up when he lights a match.

Alpine Climbers (MM cartoon)
The gang confronts beastly mountain denizens. Pluto ties one on with a St. Bernard; Donald saves the day.

Mickey's Circus (MM cartoon)
Donald reaches new heights of fury on the high wire and matches wits with a trained seal.

Donald and Pluto (MM cartoon)
After unknowingly swallowing a magnet dropped by Donald (a plumber), Pluto tries to overcome his mysterious attractiveness.

1937

Don Donald (MM cartoon)
Donald trades his faithful burro in for a car to impress Donna (later Daisy) Duck. The burro triumphs.

Magician Mickey (MM cartoon)
Unsuccessful at heckling Mickey, Donald grabs a magic pistol and starts a riot.

Moose Hunters (MM cartoon)
Goofy and Donald dress as decoy moose; Mickey is hunter. Real moose appears to battle with all three.

Mickey's Amateurs (MM cartoon)
A jeering audience greets Donald's recitation on Mickey's radio show. Clara Cluck, Clarabelle, and Goofy also perform.

Modern Inventions (MM cartoon)
Donald's misadventures amid a museum of mechanical gadgets and robots.

Hawaiian Holiday (MM cartoon)
Tropical topics for Mickey, Donald, and Goofy—sun, sand, and sea, and the funniest hula ever danced.

Clock Cleaners (MM cartoon)
Those daring young men—Mickey, Donald, and Goofy—on a sky-high clock tower.

Donald's Ostrich
Donald, a station agent, discovers an ostrich who swallows his radio.

Lonesome Ghosts (MM cartoon)
Mickey, Donald, and Goofy—professional ghost exterminators—get summoned to a haunted house by some bored and lonely spirits.

1938

Self Control
Donald, beset by outdoor pests, struggles to contain his rage, but at last smashes radio he's been listening to (program is on self-control).

Boat Builders (MM cartoon)
Mickey, Donald, and Goofy build a folding boat that collapses as soon as it's launched.

Donald's Better Self
Play hooky or go to school? Donald must choose between the exhortations of his Evil Self and his Better Self.

Orphan's Picnic (1936).

Donald's Nephews
Donald tries to practice child psychology on prankster nephews Huey, Dewey, and Louie.

Mickey's Trailer (MM cartoon)
Gags on the road with Mickey, Donald, and Goofy when their trailer becomes separated from their car.

Polar Trappers
At the South Pole, a walrus and a penguin colony elude the wiles of Donald and Goofy.

*Good Scouts
On a scouting expedition with his nephews, Donald runs afoul of a bear and gets caught in a geyser.

The Fox Hunt
Riding to the hounds, Donald finds himself holed up with the fox.

The Whalers (MM cartoon)
A perilous hunt for Mickey, Donald, and Goofy— Mickey saves his friends from becoming modern Jonahs.

Donald's Golf Game
Donald is handicapped by the machinations of Huey, Dewey, and Louie.

1939

Donald's Lucky Day
Messenger boy Donald delivers a live bomb on Friday the 13.

Hockey Champ
Donald shows off hockey skill to nephews, who challenge him and beat him at his own game.

Donald's Cousin Gus
The arrival of the goose who makes a pig of himself.

Beach Picnic
A trouble-filled day at the seashore for Donald and Pluto.

Sea Scouts
The Duck, a great navigator, sails into the middle of a shark fight.

Donald's Penguin
Donald receives a troublesome penguin as a gift. He is about to shoot the bird when it disappears. Later, an affectionate reunion.

The Autograph Hound
On a movie set, police chase Donald. So do the stars who want his autograph. Caricatures of Garbo, Rooney, Temple, Ritz Brothers and Armetta.

Officer Duck
Donald poses as a baby on a doorstep to serve eviction papers on Pete.

1940

The Riveter
Riveting gives Donald the jitters, but not more so than his menacing boss, Pete.

Donald's Dog Laundry
The story of Donald the drip-dry duck begins as he tries to entice Pluto into his mechanical dog washer.

Tugboat Mickey (MM cartoon)
Mickey, Donald, and Goofy's frantic scramble to answer an SOS.

Billposters
A hungry goat becomes the nemesis of billposters Donald and Goofy.

Mr. Duck Steps Out
Donald's date with Daisy is ruined by his nephews.

Put-Put Troubles
Motorboating leads Donald and Pluto to a watery finale.

Donald's Vacation
The Duck on holiday with reluctant folding-camp equipment, thieving chipmunks, and an unfriendly bear.

Window Cleaners
High comedy and disaster for Donald and his sleepy helper, Pluto.

Fire Chief
Donald sets fire to his own station house and then douses it with gasoline instead of water.

The Vanishing Private
Since Donald has camouflaged himself, it appears to the General that Pete is chasing nothing. General puts Pete in a straitjacket and orders Donald to guard him.

1941

Timber
Donald (with an ax to grind) feuds with Pierre and leads him on a mad railroad handcar chase.

Golden Eggs
Disguised as a chicken, Donald tries to recover eggs protected by a rooster.

A Good Time for a Dime
Donald's ill-fortune in a penny arcade.

The Nifty Nineties (MM cartoon)
Mickey and Minnie attend an old-time vaudeville show. Donald Duck rides by on a bicycle in a cameo role.

Early to Bed
Donald's loudly ticking alarm clock keeps him awake; his efforts to get rid of it backfire.

*Truant Officer Donald
Donald tries to smoke hooky-playing nephews out of a shack and then weeps over three burnt roast chickens he mistakes for their corpses. Nephews get back to school in time for vacation.

Orphan's Benefit
A color remake of the 1934 cartoon.

Old MacDonald Duck
To the accompaniment of "Old MacDonald's Farm" Donald undertakes routine farm chores.

Donald's Camera
A woodpecker's interference with Donald's photography causes him to substitute gunshots for snapshots.

Chef Donald
Donald dons his toque blanche to whip up a batch of rubber-cement waffles.

The Village Smithy
The Duck encounters frustration in trying to shoe a donkey.

Mickey's Birthday Party (MM cartoon)
The gang surprises Mickey with a jam session and a burnt cake.

1942

Symphony Hour (MM cartoon)
Mickey's radio orchestra gives a gadget band performance; sponsor Pete becomes irate.

Donald's Snow Fight
For smashing their snowman, the nephews assault Donald with snowballs containing mousetraps.

Donald Gets Drafted
Donald's ordeal at his Army physical, in boot camp, on KP duty.

Donald's Garden
Gophers threaten Donald's prizewinning watermelon crop.

Donald's Gold Mine
As a hapless miner, Donald tangles with machinery and is compressed into a gold brick.

The Vanishing Private
Since Donald has camouflaged himself, it appears to the General that Pete is chasing nothing.

Sky Trooper
The intrepid Duck tries to parachute—and falls right into KP duty.

Bellboy Donald
Serving Senator Pete, Donald loses his temper when the Senator's bratty son taunts him.

1943

****Der Fuehrer's Face*
In a satiric nightmare, Donald envisions his existence as a Nazi.

Donald's Tire Trouble
Four blowouts and Donald blows up.

Flying Jalopy
Donald's rattletrap plane is attacked by its former owner (Ben Buzzard) who has made out Donald's insurance to himself.

Fall Out—Fall In
Private Duck endures a long, wearying march, has trouble with his tent, and gets to sleep just when it's time to "fall in."

The Old Army Game
Using a record of snoring sounds, Private Duck executes a daring plan to escape Pete.

Home Defense
With a toy airplane and parachutist, Huey, Dewey, and Louie trick Donald who has fallen asleep at his listening post.

1944

Trombone Trouble
The gods Jupiter and Vulcan enlist Donald to rid themselves of Pete's sour trombone playing.

Donald Duck and the Gorilla
Things get hairy when Donald mistakes the zoo's escaped gorilla for Huey, Dewey, and Louie in a monkey suit.

Contrary Condor
A climb in the Andes leads Donald to adoption by an undiscerning mother condor.

Commando Duck
Out of the sky comes the brave and fearless Army duck with instructions to destroy an enemy airfield.

The Plastics Inventor
Donald bakes his own airplane following radio instructions. It flies—until a rainstorm melts it.

Donald's Off Day
Everything goes awry on Donald's golf day; Huey, Dewey, and Louie conspire to make it worse.

1945

The Clock Watcher
Donald as a lazy gift wrapper in a toy store.

The Eyes Have It
Experimenting with hypnosis, Donald puts himself in a trance and then makes Pluto behave as a mouse, a turtle, a chicken, and a lion.

Home Defense (1943).

*Donald's Crime
Flat broke, Donald robs the nephews' piggy bank for a date with Daisy.

Duck Pimples
Characters in the whodunit Donald is reading come to life and entangle him in the plot.

No Sail
At sea in a rented boat with a coin-operated motor, Donald and Goofy run out of nickels.

Cured Duck
At Daisy's insistence, Donald takes a course to learn how to control his temper.

Old Sequoia
Forest ranger Donald does his best to protect a redwood from hungry beavers.

1946

Donald's Double Trouble
Donald employs a look-alike to help him win back Daisy's love.

Wet Paint
In between heckling from a bird, Donald tries to paint his roadster.

Dumb Bell of the Yukon
Trapper Donald on the trail of a fur coat for Daisy.

Lighthouse Keeping
Donald battles annoying birds, who try to douse his lighthouse's flame.

Frank Duck Brings 'Em Back Alive
Safari adventure à la King Kong: Donald attempts to capture the "wildman of the jungle"—Goofy.

1947

Straight Shooters
The nephews disguise themselves as a princess and then a mummy to trick Donald, a barker in a shooting gallery.

Sleepy Time Donald
After sleepwalking to her house, Donald is escorted home by Daisy. He awakens and accuses her of sleepwalking.

Clown of the Jungle
The crazy singing and dancing Aracuan bird (first seen in *Saludos Amigos*) drives Donald to distraction by ruining his attempts to photograph jungle wildlife.

Donald's Dilemma
After a blow on the head turns Donald into a great singer, Daisy consults a psychiatrist to cope with the possibility of losing him to fame.

Crazy With the Heat
Mirages of soda fountains, icebergs, and a polar bear appear to Donald and Goofy, stranded in the desert.

Bootle Beetle
Donald's search for a runaway beetle he wants to add to his bug collection.

Wide Open Spaces
Donald stops at a motel he can't afford and ends up asleep in a cactus bed.

*Chip 'n' Dale
Needing firewood, Donald chops down Chip 'n' Dale's home. The ingenious chipmunks later reclaim their log from the fireplace.

1948

Drip Dippy Donald
A dripping faucet keeps Donald awake; the next morning a phone call informs him the water is being turned off until bill is paid.

Daddy Duck
Donald becomes guardian to a playful kangaroo.

Donald's Dream Voice
"Ajax Voice Pills" transform Donald into an irresistible supersalesman.

The Trial of Donald Duck
On a rainy day, Donald takes his lunch into a swanky restaurant and orders only coffee. For refusing to pay the fantastic charge, he's sentenced to wash dishes.

Inferior Decorator
The flowered wallpaper Donald is hanging attracts a bee, who becomes enraged.

Soup's On
The nephews get punished for not washing up before dinner. As part of their revenge they make Donald think he's died and become an angel.

Three for Breakfast
Chip 'n' Dale "harpoon" pancakes in Donald's kitchen. Their last catch—a rubber-cement cake.

*Tea for Two Hundred
It's no picnic for Donald when an army of ants throw him in the river and steal his food.

1949

Donald's Happy Birthday
Donald forces nephews to smoke the cigars he's found in their possession, then discovers a birthday card to himself in the bottom of the box.

Sea Salts
Donald and Bootle Beetle reminisce about being shipwrecked together.

Winter Storage
Chip 'n' Dale vie with Donald for a sack of acorns.

Honey Harvester
A bee stores his honey in Donald's car radiator.

All in a Nutshell
Chip 'n' Dale steal nutbutter Donald has made from nuts he stole from the chipmunks.

The Greener Yard
The story of Donald's treatment of intruders makes a hungry beetle happy to stay in his own yard.

Slide, Donald, Slide
A bee and Donald start a violent fight over radio stations: music or baseball?

***Toy Tinkers**
On Christmas Eve, Donald finds Chip 'n' Dale under his tree—playing and stealing food.

1950

Lion Around
The nephews' prank brings Donald face to face with a raging lion.

Crazy Over Daisy
Daisy snubs Donald for his cruel treatment of Chip 'n' Dale.

Trailer Horn
In a trailer camp, Donald falls prey to Chip 'n' Dale's practical jokes.

Hook, Lion and Sinker
A lion and its cub plot to steal the fish Donald has caught.

Bee at the Beach
A pesty, divebombing bee sends Donald's boat shooting into shark-infested waters.

Out on a Limb
Donald takes malicious delight in pruning Chip 'n' Dale's tree.

1951

Dude Duck
Tenderfoot Duck saddles up the most unwilling horse in the West.

Corn Chips
Donald tricks Chip 'n' Dale into shoveling snow for him.

Test Pilot Donald
Testing his jet plane, Donald contends with Dale's antics.

Lucky Number
Nephews pick up a car Donald has unknowingly won in a raffle. Donald wrecks the car, thinking it's their hot rod.

Out of Scale
As engineer of a miniature train Donald sports with Chip 'n' Dale.

Bee on Guard
To steal honey from a beehive, Donald gets the guard bee "drunk" on honey.

1952

Donald Applecore
Donald and Chip 'n' Dale trade gags in an orchard.

Let's Stick Together
Spike the Bee and Donald reminisce about their fights and stinging arguments.

Uncle Donald's Ants
A leaking bag of sugar carried by Donald causes ants to overrun his house.

Trick or Treat
Witch Hazel works her magic to help the nephews avenge Donald's Halloween trick.

1953

Don's Fountain of Youth
Traveling with nephews, Donald stops at the Fountain of Youth and tricks the kids into thinking he's a baby again.

The New Neighbor
Donald and Pete wage backyard war; at one point, TV excitedly covers the fight.

*Rugged Bear
Donald washes, shears, and naps on a "bear rug" that's still more bear than rug.

Working for Peanuts
Chip 'n' Dale steal peanuts from Dolores, the zoo elephant, and are then chased by a furious Donald.

Canvas Back Duck
Donald makes the nephews proud by proving his strength and boxing prowess at a carnival.

1954

Spare the Rod
Donald gets a lesson in child psychology from his conscience. Later he spanks the conscience for giving bad advice.

Donald's Diary
Donald's diary reveals that he's about to marry Daisy...but then he has a frightening dream about life with her that makes him change his mind.

Dragon Around
To Chip 'n' Dale, the steam shovel Donald operates too close to their home appears to be a dragon; they set out to slay it.

Grin and Bear It
In Brownstone National Park, Humphrey the Bear devises ruses to get food from tourist Donald.

Grandcanyonscope
Making a nuisance of himself in the Grand Canyon, Donald becomes involved in a frantic chase that leaves the entire canyon filled with stones.

Flying Squirrel
When a flying squirrel doesn't get his promised reward for helping Donald put up a peanut sign, a battle ensues.

1955

*No Hunting
Donald's hair-raising hunting adventure with his Grandpappy who's come to life from a painting hanging in Donald's dining room.

Bearly Asleep
Thrown out of his cave for snoring, Humphrey the Bear tries to hibernate at Donald's house.

Beezy Bear
Donald the Beekeeper vs. Humphrey the Bear, honey thief.

Up a Tree
Donald, a logger in a lumber camp, wreaks havoc on Chip 'n' Dale's home—and ultimately on his own.

1956

Chips Ahoy
Donald tries to prevent acorn hunters Chip 'n' Dale from sailing across a river in his model ship.

Cartoons not distributed as part of a series

1956

How to Have an Accident in the Home
Donald proves the wisdom of J. J. Fate's observation, "There's no place like home...to have an accident."

1959

Donald in Mathmagic Land
Journeying through a fantastic land where trees have square roots, Donald discovers the wonders of mathematics in nature, art, architecture, games, and music.

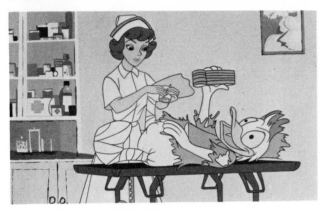

How to Have an Accident at Work
J. J. Fate returns to demonstrate Donald's carelessness on the job.

1961

Donald and the Wheel
Starting with the first circular stone and ending with space stations, Donald invents and develops the wheel.

The Litterbug
Donald gives graphic demonstrations of various types of pests—the Unconscious Carrier, Sports Bug, Sneak Bug, Highway Bug, Beach Bug, and Mountain Bug.

1967

Scrooge McDuck and Money
Advising his nephews on how to become wealthy, the world's richest duck explains the history of money and basic economics. He charges 3 cents for his advice, "for nothing good is ever free."

FEATURES

1941

The Reluctant Dragon
On a tour of the Disney Studio, Robert Benchley views, among other things, Ducky Nash recording Donald's voice and an animated scene from *Old MacDonald Duck*. A live-action animation film.

1943

Saludos Amigos
Four cartoons linked together by live-action film of Disney and his staff visiting South America. Donald Duck stars in "Lake Titicaca" and "Aquarela Do Brasil."

1945

The Three Caballeros
In this lively musical fantasy, Donald's birthday gifts—a movie projector and a book—transport him south of the border with José Carioca and Panchito.

1947

Fun and Fancy Free
The second half of this film features Edgar Bergen narrating "Mickey and the Beanstalk." Donald plays a starving peasant in a reworking of the famous tale of Jack and the Beanstalk.

1948

Melody Time
Seven sequences of live action and animation. "Blame It on the Samba" brings back Joe Carioca and the Aracuan bird to teach Donald to samba.

Donald's Decision (1941).

COMMERCIAL FILMS

1939

The Standard Parade (Standard Oil Co.)
Donald takes part in a parade bearing lettered flags that spell out the name of the company.

1940

The Volunteer Worker (Community Chests and Councils, Inc.) Doors slam in Donald's face on his house-to-house campaign for charity.

1941

Donald's Decision (National Film Board of Canada)

All Together (Nat'l Film Board of Canada)

1942

The New Spirit (U.S. Treasury. Distributed by War Activities Committee of Motion Picture Industry) Moved by "the new spirit," Donald pays his taxes promptly and sees them used to buy guns, planes, and ships "to bury the Axis."

1943

The Spirit of '43 (U.S. Treasury)
Donald decides to save his money for taxes instead of splurging on entertainment. Second half of cartoon uses same propaganda footage as *The New Spirit*.

1965

Steel and America (American Iron and Steel Institute)
The story of steel from ore to finished product.

1966

Donald's Fire Survival Plan (Educational release)
Donald shows how to plan against loss of home and life by fire.

SHORTS RELEASED FROM FEATURES

"Lake Titicaca" (*Saludos Amigos*)

"La Piñata" (*The Three Caballeros*)

"Baia" (*The Three Caballeros*)

"Mickey and the Beanstalk" (*Fun and Fancy Free*)

"Blame It on the Samba" (*Melody Time*)

DONALD DUCK TV SHOWS

1954

The Donald Duck Story (11/17/54)

A Present for Donald (1954 Christmas Show) (12/22/54)

1956

A Day in the Life of Donald Duck (2/1/56)

At Home with Donald Duck (also called *Happy Birthday, Donald Duck*) (11/21/56)

1957

Your Host, Donald Duck (1/16/57)

Donald's Award (3/27/57)

Duck for Hire (10/23/57)

1958

Donald's Weekend (1/15/58)

1959

Duck Flies Coop (2/13/59)

1960

Two Happy Amigos (2/5/60)

This Is Your Life, Donald Duck (3/11/60)

Donald's Silver Anniversary (11/13/60)

1961

Donald in Mathmagic Land (second half of *An Adventure in Color*) (9/24/61)

Inside Donald Duck (11/5/61)

Kids Is Kids (also called *Donald Duck Quacks Up*) (12/10/61)

1962

Why Man Is His Own Worst Enemy (also called *Ducking Disaster With Donald and His Friends*) (10/21/62)

1963

A Square Peg in a Round Hole (also called *Goofing Around With Donald Duck*) (3/3/63)

Trivia Quiz

1. What was Donald's favorite pet name for Daisy?

2. How many buttons were there on Donald's original middy blouse?

3. What crime did Huey, Dewey, and Louie commit in *Lost in the Andes*?

4. What did Donald have to do to become a maharajah?

5. Why did Uncle Scrooge become disenchanted with his life in *Scrooge and the Seven Cities*?

6. Who were the Larkies?

7. What color and denomination was the rare stamp Donald sought in *The Gilded Man*?

8. What was Scrooge's Christmas present to the nephews in *A Letter to Santa*?

9. How many of Donald's films were nominated for Oscars? Did any of them win an Academy Award?

10. In Carl Barks's comics, how were humans usually portrayed?

11. What model car did Donald win in *Lucky Number*?

12. Where did Chef Donald get his waffle recipe?

13. What song from a famous Disney feature did Donald sing in *The Riveter*?

14. What was "the fight of the century"?

15. True or false: Donald Duck once met the Lone Ranger.

16. In *Saludos Amigos*, what sport did Donald plan to play when he reached Venezuela?

17. To which famous movie star/sex symbol did Walt Disney compare Donald?

18. What tune did Donald play on his fife in *The Band Concert*?

19. How did the Wise Little Hen make her requests for help?

20. When and where did Scrooge get his red broadcloth coat?

21. Did Donald ever grow a beard?

22. Which two dances was Donald especially good at?

23. Does Donald Duck have a star on Hollywood Boulevard?

24. In what 1950 film did George Sanders mention Donald?

25. How hot is Donald's temper?

Answers

1. "Toots."

2. Four.

3. They blew round bubble gum bubbles in a land where everything—including the chickens—was square.

4. Ride an elephant into the kingdom of Bumpsy.

5. He became unhappy because there was nothing left for him to buy.

6. Evil creatures (based on the mythological Harpies) who captured Donald in Golden Fleecing.

7. The 1-cent magenta stamp of British Guiana.

8. A real, full-size steam shovel. Donald wanted the boys to think it was from Santa but Scrooge insisted on credit.

9. Six: Good Scouts (1938); Der Fuehrer's Face (1943); Chip 'n' Dale (1947); Tea for Two Hundred (1948); Toy Tinkers (1949); Rugged Bear (1953). Only Der Fuehrer's Face, in 1943.

10. As animal-faced characters.

11. The Zoom V-8.

12. From "Mother Mallard's Cooking Program."

13. "Heigh Ho" from Snow White and the Seven Dwarfs.

14. Donald's bout with The New Neighbor.

15. True. The masked man wanted the Duck's autograph in The Autograph Hound.

16. Golf. He brought his clubs with him.

17. Walt sometimes called Donald "the Gable of our stable."

18. "Turkey in the Straw."

19. She sang—and had a backup group, too!

20. In Scotland in 1902, The Golden Fleecing. When this story was originally published in 1954/55, the date given was 1902. When it was later reprinted, the date was changed so Scrooge wouldn't seem impossibly old.

21. Not deliberately, but he sported whiskers after being stranded at sea in No Sail.

22. The jitterbug and the samba.

23. No. Nor are there any webbed footprints in front of Grauman's Chinese Theater.

24. All About Eve. He was discoursing on the magic of the theatre.

25. Very. When Mickey Rooney threw an egg in Donald's face (in The Autograph Hound) it fried as he burned in rage.

Bibliography

Books

Arseni, Ercole. *Walt Disney's Magic Moments.* New York: Mondadori, 1973.

Bain, David, and Harris, Bruce, eds. *Mickey Mouse: Fifty Happy Years.* New York: Harmony, 1977.

Boatner, E. B. "Carl Barks—from Burbank to Calisota." *The Comic Book Price Guide #7.* New York: Harmony, 1977.

Feild, R. D. *The Art of Walt Disney.* New York: Macmillan, 1942.

Finch, Christopher. *The Art of Walt Disney: From Mickey Mouse to the Magic Kingdoms.* New York: Abrams, 1975.

Maltin, Leonard. *The Disney Films.* New York: Crown, 1973.

Munsey, Cecil. *Disneyana: Walt Disney Collectibles.* New York: Hawthorn, 1974.

Overstreet, Robert M., ed. *The Comic Book Price Guide #9.* New York: Harmony, 1979.

Schickel, Richard. *The Disney Version.* New York: Avon, 1969.

Articles

"The Ascendancy of Mr. Donald Duck." *New York Times,* June 23, 1940.

Barrier, Mike. "The Lord of Quackly Hall." *Comic Art 7,* 1967.

Burnet, Dana. "The Rise of Donald Duck." *Pictorial Review,* October 1935.

Crowther, Bosley. "Dizzy Disney: 'The Three Caballeros' Shows Brilliant Technique— But Is It Art?" *New York Times,* February 11, 1945.

———. *Saludos Amigos* review. *New York Times,* February 13, 1943.

———. *The Three Caballeros* review. *New York Times,* February 5, 1945.

Churchill, Douglass. "Now Mickey Mouse Enters Art's Temple." *New York Times Magazine,* June 3, 1934.

Ciotti, Paul. "The Man Who Drew Ducks." *California,* November 1977.

Daugherty, Frank. "How Donald Comes Out of the Paint Pots." *Christian Science Monitor,* December 14, 1940.

"Disney Family." *Time,* April 16, 1935.

Fleming, Joseph B. "Meet Herr Donald Duck— Continental Celebrity." *Miami Herald,* June 14, 1977.

Harmetz, Aljean. "Disney Incubating New Artists." *New York Times,* July 27, 1978.

Hiss, Tony, and McClelland, David. "The Quack and Disney." *The New Yorker,* December 29, 1975.

"Honor Where Due." *New York Times,* June 13, 1938.

Maloney, Russell. "The Current Cinema." *The New Yorker*, August 13, 1938.

McGuire, Michael. "Carl Barks and the Donald Duck Gestalt." *The Daily Iowan*, December 5, 1974.

Morrison, Patt. "Fame Never Spoiled Famous Voice of Donald Duck." *Los Angeles Times*, May 16, 1976.

"New Walt Disney Artists Are Taught Animation." *The New York Times*, April 26, 1936.

Paul, Bill. "Donald Duck Faces a Morals Charge in Western Europe." *Wall Street Journal*, February 10, 1978.

Peters, Arlen. "Billygoat Act Ended Up As a Duck." (Van Nuys) *Valley News*, August 23, 1977.

Seldes, Gilbert. "No Art, Mr. Disney?" *Esquire*, September 1937.

"A Silver Anniversary for Walt and Mickey." *Life*, November 2, 1953.

Spicer, Bill. "A Visit with Carl Barks." *Graphic Story World*, July 1971.

Strauss, Theodore. "Donald Duck's Disney." *New York Times*, February 7, 1943.

Styron, Steve. "Collecting Carl Barks, 'The Good Artist.'" *Mickey's Monthly*, May 1978.

Thompson, Don, ed. "The Duck Man." *Comic Art* 7.

Thompson, Helen G. "Wanna Fight?" *Stage*, May 1936.

Tobin, Richard. "The Rise of Donald Duck." *New York Herald Tribune*, January 12, 1936.

Wagner, Dave. "Donald Duck: An Interview." *Radical America* 7 (1973).

Wallace, Irving. "Mickey Mouse and How He Grew." *Collier's*, April 9, 1949.

"Why Donald Duck Is Irresistible Even on the Radio." *Living Age*, July 1939.

The original "Duckster." Walt Disney used this to honor staff members and others for special achievements.